REA

ACPL ITEM
DISCA

SO-AUF-255

FEB 2 6 2004

The Shah and the Ayatollah

THE SHAH AND THE AYATOLLAH

Iranian Mythology and Islamic Revolution

Fereydoun Hoveyda

A National Committee on American Foreign Policy Study

Westport, Connecticut
London

Library of Congress Cataloging-in-Publication Data

Hoveyda, Fereydoun.
    The Shah and the Ayatollah : Iranian mythology and Islamic Revolution /
Fereydoun Hoveyda.
        p. cm.
    "A National committee of American Foreign Policy study."
    Includes bibliographical references and index.
    ISBN 0–275–97858–3 (alk. paper)
        1. Iran—Politics and government—1941–1979.   2. Iran—Politics and
government—1979–1997.   3. Mythology, Iranian.   4. Islam and politics—Iran.
I. Title
DS318 .H675 2003
955.05′3—dc21   2002029763

British Library Cataloguing in Publication Data is available.

Copyright © 2003 by Fereydoun Hoveyda

All rights reserved. No portion of this book may be
reproduced, by any process or technique, without the
express written consent of the publisher.

Library of Congress Catalog Card Number: 2002029763
ISBN: 0–275–97858–3

First published in 2003

Praeger Publishers, 88 Post Road West, Westport, CT 06881
An imprint of Greenwood Publishing Group, Inc.
www.praeger.com

Printed in the United States of America

The paper used in this book complies with the
Permanent Paper Standard issued by the National
Information Standards Organization (Z39.48-1984).

10 9 8 7 6 5 4 3 2 1

Copyright Acknowledgment
The author and publisher gratefully acknowledge permission from Mage Publishers Inc. to reprint excerpts from Dick Davis' *Father and Sons*. Washington, DC,
2000.

Contents

Preface

As far back as I remember, I was always steeped in Iranian mythology. I was three years old, in Damascus. My mother and the servants who had been brought from Iran would tell me the deeds and fates of our legendary kings and heroes. To them these fearless champions had really existed and were part of our history. Hence my surprise when in grade two in the French Lycée of Beirut (I was six years old) I noticed that our teacher did not mention them in his version of Iran's history. To my query she answered: "Oh that! It's mythology!" At home my nanny shrugged her shoulders: "Your teacher is an ignorant! Don't listen to her!" Years passed on and we schoolkids became acquainted with Greek mythology and other legends. But I discovered that they were not told at home to European kids and at any rate their legends were very different from ours. For one thing, they referred to multiple gods who were not always morally right like our Wise Lord who continuously fought against Ahriman, the evil spirit.

Thus the difference between Iran and the rest of the world struck and intrigued me since my early years. But, as it happens, I forgot about it after I entered secondary school. It was much later that my childhood memories popped back in my mind. While reading Freud in the late 1940s, I felt somehow at odds with his theories about the Oedipus complex. I remembered our story of the superman Rostam, inadvertently killing his son Sohrab. I then started a study of other mythologies. I certainly do not pretend to be an expert, but in the course of my readings and research I have gathered enough data to convince myself of the active role these legends of the remotest past play in the present lives of people.[1] In the case of Iran, this is even more apparent as we have preserved, almost intact, the whole body of our mythology despite all the invasions and occupations to which we have been subjected over the centuries and millennia. Our legends are being continually told to kids and recounted publicly to children as well as adults. I remember a 1995 lecture given by Professor K.D. Irani, an American Parsi, to the City College's Faculty Colloquium on World Humanities. Although his subject matter concerned the influence of Indian epics on early Sanskrit drama, he explained how old legends were still kept alive by public storytellers who traveled to the remotest villages. He also told us about one of his childhood experiences in Bombay: he was ten years old when Iranian artists staged in the Opera House some of the old stories concerning Zoroaster and legendary kings such as Jamshid and Kaykhosrow.[2] Their recitations accompanied by music moved the audience to the point of weeping! Such public performances were also very common in Iran before the Islamic revolution. On the transmission of ancient mythology to kids, André Malraux reports a conversation with Nehru in which the first Indian prime minister told him, "Even ill-lettered women know our national epics and recount them to kids as bedtime stories."[3]

The part played by mothers (or nannies) in the transmission of old legends has been acknowledged by many specialists and researchers. Thus, Professor Carlo Ginzburg during his research came across the trial of a sixteenth-century shepherd of a village north of Venice, who claimed that on certain nights, armed with fennel sticks, he and his fellow villagers battled with the devil's witches for the fertility of their farmlands. He told an American interviewer: "The case was reminiscent of a fairy tale and I immediately reacted to it. It was like the Sicilian fable my mother read to me as a child. Those fairy tales molded my mind and emotions."[4]

At any rate, I have found many points in the events that led to the fall of Muhammad Reza Shah and the ascent of Ayatollah Khomeini that can be explained only by the impact of old mythology on Iranians' mind-sets.[5] I have tried to develop them in the present book in the hope that my narrative will trigger further studies.

CHAPTER ONE

The Shah and the Ayatollah

Iran's 1979 Islamic revolution was in a way the outcome of a long struggle between two men: Shah Muhammad Reza Pahlavi and Ayatollah Ruhollah Khomeini. In 1963, following rioting provoked by the latter, the Shah won what can be considered as the first round: he arrested his nemesis and later on exiled him. Sixteen years later the ayatollah triumphed in the second round and returned to Iran after the flight of his enemy.

Each of them represented (at least partially) one of the basic and contradictory trends that had agitated the nation since the early years of the twentieth century: secularist modernization on the one hand and religious orthodoxy and traditionalism on the other. Their individual personalities and the "archetypes" with which they identified had a great bearing on the turn of events, especially because Iran is a country where the patriarchal structure of society remained solid and active. Therefore a quick look at their biographies might shed light on some of the unexplained aspects of Iran's turmoils and predicaments during the last decades of the twentieth century. At any rate, as in a wrestling match, let us start by briefly introducing the combatants.

KHOMEINI'S TRAJECTORY

The name of the ayatollah means: native of Khomein, a small rural town in the province of Esfahan which did not attract mullahs, who are generally interested in more lush and materially profitable places. The local landowner could not find a religious man who would help him keep his farmers in check. While on pilgrimage in Najaf (holy Shiite city in Iraq) he met Ruhollah's grandfather, a rather indigent cleric whose ancestors had migrated to India from Neyshapour (a northeastern Iranian town). The landowner, impressed by the mullah's title of *seyed* (descendant of the Prophet), lured him with the offer of a house and some land. The family left India and settled in Khomein, where Ruhollah was born, around 1901.

In those days Iran was in a state of great chaos and turbulence. Russian influence extended to the North and British influence to the south of the country. Tribal chieftains and feudal khans (landowners) swayed power in their domains. Brigands infested roads and trails, cutting almost all contacts between the provinces and the capital city of Tehran where the absolutist Qajar kings ruled. In 1905, a motley group composed of young modernists, intellectuals, aristocrats, landowners, high-ranking clerics, and some bazaar merchants took advantage of the weakening of central authority in order to impose a parliamentary constitutional regime on the Shah.

The traditionalists reacted almost immediately against this import to Muslim Iran of institutions created by the Western infidels. The most vocal among them, Hojat-ol-Islam Nouri, author of several books and pamphlets about djinns and other demons, invited the Iranians to revolt against the modernists. "Wake up," he repeated in his sermons, "Islam is in danger! What we need is not a parliament and a constitution, but an Islamic government." His criticism of high-ranking mullahs favoring the constitutional reform provoked the ire of top clerics who accused him of heresy and sent him to an Islamic tribunal. He was condemned to death for "warring against God" (Today's Iranian Islamic courts accuse modernists of the same "crime"!). Hojat-ol-Islam Nouri was eventually hanged in a public place with the enthusiastic approval of the crowds. Fearing a similar fate, fundamentalist mullahs fled from the capital and hid in the provinces where they opened Koranic schools. (Ruhollah Khomeini became a pupil in one such school.)

Ruhollah's father died shortly after his birth in a brawl with the intendants of the local feudal landowner. His destitute and pregnant widow put the infant in the care of her sister who had married a wealthy merchant. In the household of his aunt, the boy learned the importance of vengeance, a character trait that would undergird his long fight against the Shah. One of the biographies spread after the 1979 revolution insisted on the fact that he was brought up by his aunt and uncle because of the parallel with Prophet Muhammad's life. Indeed, the latter became an orphan at an early age and lived with his aunt and uncle![1] But at the time of his birth people dubbed Khomeini as *badghadam* (bird of ill-omen), because of the coincidence of his birth with the tragic death of his father.[2] As a result, the villagers avoided him and when they couldn't, recited Koranic verses or other incantations in order to exorcise demons and ward off dangers.[3]

Abandoned by his real mother, shunned by the people, the child focused his love on his aunt who used to say on all occasions that Islam could not flourish by sermons and speeches alone, but only through an all-out jihad (holy war) against its adversaries. When he reached the age of five, his uncle sent him to a Koranic school.

Ruhollah was 15 when his mother and aunt passed away. As he had finished his Koranic school, nothing retained him anymore in his birthplace. He left Khomein for the nearest city, Arak, where a disciple of the dissident Hojat-ol-Islam Nouri taught theology. Khomeini, who already entertained the ambition of climbing the clerical ladder to its top, enrolled in this school and probably heard there for the first time about the establishment of an Islamic government. After a short stay in Arak, moved by ambition, he left for the holy city of Qum where many great scholars resided and directed the most prestigious Shiite seminars. In the meantime, World War I had prompted the Russians, the British, and, later on, the Turks to occupy parts of the country. Travelling became almost impossible and the young Khomeini bided his time and studied theology.

BIRTH OF A FUTURE KING

On October 26, 1919, in a very modest Tehran house, a few months before Khomeini's move to Qum at age 19, Muhammad Reza, who would become his target and victim some thirty years later, came into the world. His father, Reza Khan Mirpanj, was the colonel of the cossack regiment created by the Russian counselors of the Qajar shahs.

As in the case of Khomeini, Reza Khan's father had died a couple of months after his birth, but details about his family and childhood are lacking. Later on, after his accession to the throne, Muhammad Reza vaguely pretended that his great-grandfather was a general by the name of Murad Ali Khan who had participated in the siege of Herat, Afghanistan, and his grandfather a colonel in the Qajar army.[4] This contention belies his mother's declarations to a French magazine.[5] At any rate, what is certain is that Reza Khan joined the cossacks as an illiterate footsoldier around the age of 14 and managed to learn reading and writing and to reach the rank of colonel in his mid-forties.

Muhammad Reza's childhood was a happy one but lacked any aristocratic touch. It rather resembled that of many lower-middle-class kids. But things rapidly changed, and people attributed the sudden quirk of fortune of Reza Khan to the boy's birth. They dubbed him *khoshghadam* (bird of good omen). Indeed, a year after his birth his father became the commander of the cossack brigade and later minister of war in the cabinet of *seyed* Zia-o-Din Tabatabai, after the 1921 coup d'etat. The Shah Ahmad Qajar bestowed nobility on the family by giving Reza Khan the title of *Sardar Sepah* (marshal of the army) and his wife that of *Taj-ol-Molouk* (crown of kings).

The clergy did not approve of the new prime minister: a *seyed* (descendant of the Prophet) should not don a European frock coat and talk of modernizing the country! But, like bazaar merchants and the majority of the public, they backed Reza Khan who appeared as a strong man capable of restoring order and security and stemming the danger of the Bolshevik revolution which loomed in the northern provinces (a communist republic had even been proclaimed in Guilan by Mirza Kutchik Khan who boasted of close relations with Lenin). Three months after the coup, Reza Khan replaced Prime Minister *seyed* Zia-o-Din who resigned and fled to English-ruled Palestine. A couple of years later, Reza Khan convinced Ahmad Shah to travel to Europe and thus became practically the sole ruler of the nation. His vision was to depose the Qajar Shah and proclaim a republic as Mustafa Kemal Ataturk had done in Turkey. But the clergy, afraid of Ataturk's secularist regime, persuaded him to abandon his idea and instead become Shah. Consumed by ambition, Reza Khan did not hesitate to follow their suggestion.[6]

As a result, by age six, Muhammad Reza became crown prince of Iran. Obviously his life underwent a complete transformation as in a fairy tale! He quit the modest family home for the royal palace where he wallowed in luxury, but he could never forget his humble origins. Most probably this basic contradiction was instrumental in developing megalomania in his character—but let's not anticipate.

APPRENTICESHIP OF A MULLAH

Upon his arrival in Qum, the young Khomeini discretely inspected the seminars and sized up the teachers. He was looking for a materially and spiritually well-off master. High-ranking clerics usually receive substantial donations, according to Koranic rules, from wealthy believers. These "Islamic taxes" allow them to provide for their families and the students they enroll in their seminars. After a few days of search and reflection, he felt attracted to Sheikh Abdulkarim Haeri, who kept a modest lifestyle despite his great renown and his high income. Khomeini presented himself to the illustrious *faghih* and was accepted. Right from the start he tried to emulate the ascetic manners of the old cleric and rapidly won his confidence through extreme deference and performance of practical services. In less than a few months he became indispensable to his master.

In those days (early 1920s), many Caucasus Shiites running away from the Bolshevik revolution flocked to Qum. They told at length about the savage persecution of Muslims at the hands of the communists. They contended that Lenin and his underlings acted at the behest of Zionists who wanted to establish a world Jewish government and eradicate Islam. Their stories profoundly impressed the young Khomeini and reminded him of his aunt's views concerning the necessity of fighting infidels. Anti-Semitism started to creep into his mind, and many years later the rumors heard in his youth appeared almost word for word in one of his major works. In *Kashfol-Asrar* (Unveiling of the Mysteries) one can find, among other affirmations, the following sentence: "The Jews and their backers have in mind to destroy Islam and establish a world Jewish government."

At the same time, many rumors were circulating in Qum about Tehran's coup d'etat and *seyed* Zia-o-Din's premiership. As much as the religious establishment of the holy city despised the *seyed* who had betrayed his forebears and the Prophet, they hoped that the new war minister Reza Khan would restore order and combat the communists and their allies. The city heavily felt the toll of disorder and absence of security: the activity of bandits on roads and trails had dangerously diminished commerce and the number of pilgrims, which represented the main source of its inhabitants' income. Reza Khan, the strong man of the cabinet, was deemed a savior! But the sympathy towards him did not last long because as soon as he acceded to the throne he heralded a nationalistic program highlighting Iran's pre-Islamic civilization and achievements. The clerics construed this as a new conspiracy against Islam concocted by Westerners and Jews. In order to gain the attention and sympathy of Qum's religious dignitaries, the young Khomeini composed a pamphlet in which he wrote that before Islam, Iran suffered from ignorance and the cruelty of its rulers. He added, "There is nothing worth glorification in the pre-Islamic past of the country."[7]

In his theological studies he was attracted by the life of the 12 Imams, direct descendants of the Prophet. He was particularly impressed by their patience and by their contempt for worldly riches. They had valiantly resisted the continuous persecutions of their Sunnite enemies and kept intact their faith and the secret knowledge bestowed on them by their fathers. Having himself suffered during his childhood because of the tragic death of his father, he started a process of identification with the Saint Imams and other heroes of Shiite Islam. He used to ponder on the similitudes with his own life he could find in their biographies and dreamed of formidable actions against the enemies of the Shiite faith.

The young seminarist was appalled by the decrees issued by the new Shah such as the following: wearing European costumes, banning the *chador* (women's veil), imposing the military draft, and secularizing education and justice (previously in the hands of the clergy). To his fellow students he proposed to fight against the central government. But his master, Sheikh Abdulkarim Haeri, opposed the use of violence and favored restraint and prudence. "Let's wait and see," he used to repeat to his pupils and followers. Khomeini learned to restrain his impulses and to bide his time. This experience would serve him later to withstand crises and misfortunes without giving up his determination and pugnacity.

While Reza Shah was accelerating the pace of his reforms, Khomeini had to return to Arak for the interment of the father of one of his closest friends. He found out there that the police, in their eagerness to obey the Shah's orders, pushed things so far as to force mullahs in large cities to shave their beards and abandon their turbans. He decided to remain in Arak until the zeal of law enforcement officers would subside. But days passed and absence from Qum could delay his ascension of the clerical ladder. Superstitious as all Iranians, he consulted a dervish known for his knowledge of the occult and his divinatory powers. The old man assured him that no immediate danger menaced him and that he would die at a very old age in Qum. The young Ruhollah returned to Qum travelling by night in order to hide his mullah's garb and avoid law enforcers.

THE MAKING OF A SHAH

Since the coronation of his father as *Shahinshah* (king of kings) who adopted the family name Pahlavi,[8] Muhammad Reza's life became a continuing dream. The title of crown prince swelled his ego. A bevy of servants were at his beck and call. High-ranking officers and ministers bowed to him, though he was a child. People truckled before him. At age eleven, he was made honorary colonel of a cavalry regiment! Nevertheless, his happiness was far from complete. He dreaded his father, whose fits and even mere frowns petrified everybody, including the members of his own family.

Reza Khan did not change his lifestyle and wonts. He remained the frugal soldier he had always been. He continued to don his military uniform and slept on a mattress laid on the floor. He wanted to make out of his son a strong leader like himself, but Muhammad

Reza was rather weak if not cowardly. He disliked the military school to which he was sent. Moreover, in his eagerness to keep him on the right track, his father never missed an occasion to comment, often brutally, on his conduct. These continuous cutting remarks profoundly wounded the young boy. As in the case of Khomeini, contradictory character traits developed in Muhammad Reza's mind since early childhood. But he could not control them in adulthood like his nemesis. Indeed, in moments of crisis, he was struck by indecision and weakness, both in family affairs and official matters.

In 1931, Reza Shah sent the crown prince to a select Swiss secondary school for super rich and aristocrat kids. This experience marked the future monarch.[9] In his spare time he would reflect on great Iranian kings such as Cyrus and Darius. In a long interview published as a book, he pretended that Western democracies impressed him. One can doubt this contention as he affirmed, "(In) my years in Europe … I grasped the spirit of democracy, discipline, freedom and realized that discipline without democracy is authoritarianism and that democracy without discipline is anarchy."[10]

In fact, as is the case for many other Iranians, the first contact with a highly advanced Europe and the comparison with the medieval backwardness of his homeland induced a feeling of shame in the future king. Though approving the reforms started by his father, he had a much larger vision of modernization. His conception, as exemplified in the 1960s, went beyond change of costume and building of railways. But four years in Switzerland could not transform his character. Not only did the basic contradiction mentioned earlier not subside, but another one was added to it: between scientific rationalism learned in Europe and the traditional beliefs which had been implanted in his mind by his mother and the servants. Indeed, despite accusations by Khomeini and his followers, Muhammad Reza was a religious man to the point of superstition. He did not practice the rituals, but venerated the Imams who, he claimed, visited him in his dreams. He was convinced that they had saved him in his childhood and twice from attempts on his life.[11]

Upon his return from Europe in 1936, Muhammad Reza entered the military academy and became a lieutenant in 1938. He then accompanied his father on his inspection tours. On one of these trips, his father said that he wanted to improve the state's bureaucracy to such a perfect degree that should he die the next day, the entire administration would operate automatically from day to day without any need of supervision from the top. Muhammad Reza was offended and thought to himself, "What does he mean? Does he think that if he were gone, I should not be able to take over and continue his work?" His father's remark troubled the young prince, but he lacked the courage to tell him so to his face.[12]

KHOMEINI ON HIS OWN

In contrast to the future Shah, the future Ayatollah Ruhollah Khomeini did not dread any father. His had died at his birth, and his religious mentor, Sheikh Abdulkarim Haeri, was a soft-spoken moderate man. This circumstance explains the unusual determination and combativity of Khomeini in face of the "father of the nation," the Shah.

In the early 1930s, the campaign against the clergy abated as Reza Shah became interested in buying large chunks of land from the feudal landowners at discount prices fixed by himself! Khomeini took advantage of this new situation in order to accomplish the pilgrimage to the tomb of Imam Reza, one of the 12 Shiite saints buried in Mashad. On his way back, he stopped in Tehran where he married a *seyedeh* (feminine of *seyed* in the Arabic language) from a wealthy family. Upon his return to Qum, his old master, whose health was declining, entrusted him with the teaching at his seminar. The sudden promotion of Khomeini triggered criticism on the part of some of the other high-ranking clerics. Usually, theology teachers were chosen among middle-aged proven mullahs. The boost to Ruhollah's hubris was such that, at the death of his master, he tried to replace him, but higher religious authorities rejected him and he was forced to look for another master. Nevertheless, he was allowed to bear the title of *hojat-ol-Islam* (middle-rank cleric, before becoming ayatollah).

In 1935, a group of mullahs opposed to Reza Shah's reforms took refuge in the sanctuary of Imam Reza in Mashad, but the police hesitated to enter the sacred place. Some of the law enforcers, fearing the ire of the interred Imam, even joined the mullahs. Infuriated by this bout of disobedience, Reza Shah ordered the army to arrest the insurgents. The walls around the sanctuary were demolished by cannon balls and the mullahs surrendered. This incident, exaggerated through rumors, provoked a definite breaking-off between the Shah and the clergy. An earthquake north of Mashad was construed by the public as a celestial sign of disapproval of the Shah's action. The majority of city dwellers defended the mullahs in private but did not dare express any open criticism of the Shah. The masses, especially in the countryside, were not ready to follow the clergy: they hoped that modernization would improve their lot. Besides, Reza Shah's nationalism appealed to the educated classes.

Back in Qum, Khomeini prospered. Because of his *seyed*'s black turban he easily found followers among devout and superstitious people who believed that by offering a descendant of the Prophet the Koranic "donation tax," they would gain Allah's mercy and indulgence in the hereafter and a place in paradise. At the same time, the future ayatollah entered the realm of business by founding with his brother a bus line between Arak and Qum.

At age 40, Khomeini appeared as a stern and rigorous priest, pursuing relentlessly, though patiently, his fixed goals. He did not show any sign of emotion even in the most strained situation. Was this coldness in his nature or only the effect of shrewd acting? It is difficult to say. But the fact remains that when, after some fifteen years of exile, he stepped down from the plane bringing him back to Iran and a journalist asked him what he felt, he answered, "Nothing."[13] As Amir Taheri noted in his book about the ayatollah, attachment to a country constituted a sin for him: one should only love God and obey Him.[14]

In 1937, Khomeini accomplished the prescribed pilgrimage to Mecca. On his way back, he stopped in Najaf, the Shiite holy city in Iraq where he met Navab Safavi, a charismatic young fanatic who advocated the murder of the so-called enemies of Islam. Safavi was in contact with Egypt's Muslim Brotherhood and would later create a terrorist group of his own in Iran. In those days, German Nazis were active in the region and were helping an anticolonialist Iraqi movement led by Rashid Ali Queylani. Khomeini's stay in Najaf fortified him in his determination to fight against Reza Shah's anti-Islamic reforms. When in 1941 the Allies occupied Iran and forced the monarch to abdicate, Khomeini convinced a number of mullahs to accompany him to Tehran in order to oppose the continuation of the Pahlavi dynasty, but he did not find support in the capital city and returned to Qum. There he published, in 1942, the first version of *Kahf-ol-Asrar*.[15] In this booklet, Khomeini condemned those who criticized Islam and among them especially Ahmad Kasravi, a secularist historian and polemist whose books and articles were spreading among educated people. Navab Safavi took this condemnation by a high-ranking cleric such as Khomeini as tantamount to an authorization to kill the writer. He therefore ordered his underlings in the terrorist group he had set up under the name of *Fedayin-e-Islam* (martyrs of Islam) to proceed. Kasravi was stabbed to death in 1945. In the 1950s and 1960s the *Fedayin* killed two prime ministers: Razmara and Mansour.

BITTER VICTORY

Let us now turn to the Shah. The abdication of his father and his forced exile to South Africa by the British provoked contradictory feelings in the mind of Muhammad Reza, who had just been sworn in as the new Shah of Iran on September 16, 1941. He had been longing for that moment to prove his capability conducting the affairs of the state. But now that he had ascended the throne and was liberated from the tutelage and the constant remarks of Reza Shah, he did not feel completely happy. He could not forget the humiliating circumstances of his ascension to kingship. Many people were criticizing if not insulting the deposed leader; his exiled enemies were coming back; the political prisoners were freed; the feudal landowners were claiming back their confiscated lands; and the mullahs once again operated in the open.

On the other hand, the young monarch was in a way liberated. The eagle eye of his father was not fixed on him anymore. He could at last divorce king Farouk's sister who had been imposed as his wife by his father in 1939. He could hobnob with whomever he desired. In short, for the first time in his life, he was on his own. At the same time, he could not forget that the Allies had humiliated his father and many Iranians had joined in slighting him. That is probably why he postponed his own coronation for a quarter of a century: he did not want to give his father's enemies an opportunity for more attacks and derogatory remarks about the deposed sovereign. In 1967, the events of 1941 were forgotten and his White Revolution was beginning to bear fruit: he was not crowned as the son of Reza Shah but for his own achievements. It is also probably for the same reason that, in 1971, he organized the Persepolis celebration of the 2500th year of Iranian monarchy. He still could not get rid of the guilt he felt toward his defunct father, so, in 1976, he ordered the organization of numerous ceremonies in order to celebrate the 50th anniversary of the foundation of the Pahlavi dynasty by Reza Shah. He was not aware that all these excesses, triggered by his personal problems, would in the end ruin his own kingship!

Indeed, Khomeini did not fail to criticize the foolish expenses of these continuous celebrations and attacked Muhammad Reza Shah as a squanderer of national riches. In the wake of the 1971 Persepolis extravaganza, he called on mullahs and all Iranian people to revolt against the Shah whom he accused of betraying Islam. The "cult of personality" instituted by Muhammad Reza Shah profoundly irritated not only the clergy but also the intellectuals and many members of the political class. But let us not anticipate.

From 1941 to 1946 Iran was occupied by the British, the Russians, and the Americans. The Allies indirectly interfered in Iranian internal affairs not only for achieving their war goals, but also their own national interests. In the North, the Russians favored leftist movements while in the South the British manipulated the clergy because it was a good shield against Soviet expansionism. With the fall of Reza Shah, the communists had emerged from clandestinity and created the powerful and well-organized Tudeh party, to the dismay of the traditionalists and wealthy people. The Shah, although he inherited the antimullah feelings of his father, accepted the contention that religion could counterbalance leftists and he started a policy of rapprochement with high-ranking religious leaders. During Reza Shah's reign most of them had migrated to Najaf. The only high authority remaining in Iran at that time was Ayatollah Boroujerdi. The Shah's envoys convinced the latter to reside in Qum in order to restore the central holy city as the main venue of Shiite indoctrination. While Ayatollah Boroujerdi was in Tehran for a short stay, the Shah himself visited him in his residence. This gesture marked the reconciliation of the crown with the religious leadership.

In 1943, Franklin Roosevelt, Winston Churchill, and Joseph Stalin met in Tehran for coordinating the conduct of the war. Stalin alone paid a courtesy visit to the Shah, head of the host country. The Shah had to go to the Soviet Embassy where the conference was held in order to meet with the two other leaders. Touchy, like all Iranians, Muhammad Reza resented the attitude of the Western leaders. He attributed it to a deliberate act on the part of the Americans and British to belittle him. In fact, Roosevelt was a crippled man and besides, the security forces had discovered a plot against him and Churchill. Whatever the reason, the wound to Muhammad Reza's pride would never completely heal.

KHOMEINI VISITS THE SHAH

In any case, the move of Ayatollah Boroujerdi to Qum restored the importance of the holy city as a major center of Shiite theology. Khomeini, who had longed for years to attach himself to a higher religious authority to speed his climb up the clergy's ladder, leaped at the opportunity. He would spend days and nights in the ayatollah's waiting room, ready to perform any service from humble household chores to secretarial duties. As days passed he somehow became an indispensable aide to the prelate. At this juncture the secular writer and polemist Ahmad Kasravi, as previously indicated, was slain by a member of Navab Safavi's *Fedayin-e-Islam* terrorist group. The murderer was condemned to death. Khomeini, who had indirectly called for this crime in his *Kahf-ol-Asrar*, convinced his master to send him with a delegation of clerics to the Shah in order to obtain clemency for the assassin. There are no records of the meeting with the young Shah, who responded favorably to Ayatollah Boroujerdi's request. Apparently the monarch did not pay particular attention to Khomeini, who resented this indifference on the part of "Reza Khan's son" (as he and some other clerics used to call Muhammad Reza Shah from time to time).

Khomeini met a second time with the Shah at the behest of Ayatollah Boroujerdi, who needed funds in order to repair Saint Fatima's mausoleum in Qum. Again the Shah agreed to the ayatollah's demand without showing any interest in the members or the head of the delegation. Khomeini construed this inattention as a sign of personal disdain and conceived anger against the monarch. But, aware of the good relations between his master and the sovereign, he hid his feelings and did not mention the Shah's attitude in his report to the ayatollah.

In the late 1940s, Ayatollah Kashani, who had been sent into exile by the Allies because of his Nazi connections, came back to Qum. His rank in the clergy was much lower than that of Ayatollah Boroujerdi, but his views about the necessity of an Islamic government coincided with those of Khomeini. The two clerics met often and developed a close working relationship. This displeased Boroujerdi and prompted him to keep aloof from his cumbersome aide. When Dr. Mossadegh became prime minister in 1951 and pushed for the nationalization of the British-led oil company, Boroujerdi intimated to the mullahs not to interfere in political matters; nevertheless, Khomeini secretly helped Kashani, who was elected as member of parliament and, through slick maneuvering, became president of the legislative body! (as *Hojat-ol-Islam* Rafsanjani would some thirty years later!) But with the leaning of Mossadegh's National Front toward republicanism and the growth of the communist Tudeh party and its infiltration into the ranks of the army, Kashani was panic-stricken and soon abandoned the old prime minister and compromised with the Shah.

In 1953, after the overthrow of Mossadegh's government, both Boroujerdi and Kashani supported the witch hunt against the communists who had infiltrated the army and the bureaucracy. Khomeini found himself almost totally isolated. Yet he had already gained some renown as theology teacher in the *Fayzieh* seminar set up by Ayatollah Boroujerdi upon his return to Qum. Many mullah students flocked around Khomeini, and moreover, he had been able to gather a circle of followers such as Montazeri, Motaheri, Bahonar, Khalkhali, and Beheshti, whose names would rise in the 1979 Islamic revolution. His entourage called him aya-tollah, though he was only a *hojat-ol-Islam*, and they advised him to nominate representatives in major cities, like other important clerics. His students published his courses in the form of question-answer books.

In the meantime, Boroujerdi's health was failing and his peers were discretely considering the problem of his successor. Khome-ini had acted as his quasi secretary for many years and considered himself in good stead. But in order to become a grand ayatollah he had to entertain, like his ailing master, some normal if not close re-lations with the Shah and the central government. Despite his op-position to the Pahlavi dynasty, he ceased his attacks overnight.[16] It is even said that he sent messages to the royal court in order to compensate for his reputation as a radical (which could hurt his ambitions).

When the Grand Ayatollah Boroujerdi passed away, the Shah, as was customary, sent condolence cables to top clerics. Khomeini's name was not included, although the theology teacher, now in his late fifties, considered himself a high-ranking clergyman. He took the omission as a personal insult and resumed his attacks against the monarch. In fact, the sovereign and his aides were unaware of the existence of this small hyper-ambitious and spiteful ayatollah. His sudden emergence a few years later took almost everybody by sur-prise: nobody in political circles had even heard his name! Be this as it may, Khomeini's self-esteem was terribly wounded, like the Shah's in the case where Roosevelt and Churchill did not call on him in 1943. This brings me to a remark which I consider essen-tial to the understanding of the 1978–79 events: despite all the differences in their upbringing and personal character, Khomeini and the Shah were animated by a *common psychological pattern*. One can say that the omission of a condolence message and the narcissistic character of Khomeini in the mid-1950s put the fat in the fire and triggered a chain of events that proved fatal to the monarchy.

KHOMEINI MEDITATES

Having lost the battle of Boroujerdi's succession, Khomeini hid his disappointment through accomplishment of supplementary devotions. He would retreat from time to time into extended periods of meditation. He would remain sometimes forty days in his private reception room, refusing to see visitors and even members of his own family. Montazeri (who was designated after the revolution as his successor before being dismissed and confined to house arrest), was the only person authorized to cross his door and that for very short spells. Nobody can say what was going on at that time in the ayatollah's head. Did he really meditate? That is possible as he had flirted with mysticism in his youth. Did he think about plans to overthrow the Shah? This is also possible. In fact, he apparently imitated the Prophet and the Saint Imams who used to accomplish retreats during which "heaven would open its gates to them." Did Khomeini really believe that he could communicate with Allah and His angels? Did he really expect a visit from archangel Gabriel? At any rate, after the revolution his devotees pretended that during these retreats the archangel visited him as he had done with the Prophet some 1,400 years earlier; they contended that the archangel entrusted him with the divine mission of establishing an Islamic government first in Iran and then in the rest of the world.

Khomeini himself neither confirmed nor denied these affirmations; however, he often presented his actions as commanded by the Almighty. He considered himself if not the reincarnation of the Hidden Imam, at least his so-to-say licensed representative on earth.

After this period of meditation, he started to speak without ambiguity about the direct reign of the clergy at all levels of the state. In his campaign against the Shah, he used the themes of xenophobia and anti-Semitism, which corresponded to dormant feelings in the minds of the masses. His language itself tended toward oversimplification: he used popular dialect and images more often than not.

For some years, Khomeini stayed on guard, teaching his ideas to his students while inviting them to remain extremely prudent. He left the direction of the opposition against the Shah to the followers of the overthrown Dr. Mossadegh, and to other secular and liberal elements. It became evident much later that he was only shrewdly biding his time! He was waiting for the right moment to unleash his mullahs and throw them in the battlefield in order to seize all the threads of power! In the meantime, he confined himself to the problems of the religious sphere, developing his slogan of "Islam in danger" and accusing the Shah of sliding towards a revival of Zoroastrianism. He invited Iranian Muslims to mourn rather than celebrate on the occasion of the Iranian new year, the Nowrouz inherited from the pre-Islamic period, on the grounds that this was a profane non-Muslim festival, almost a pagan practice. But he was preaching in the wilderness and his appeals rarely went farther than Qum.

The Shah, on the other hand, under pressure by the Kennedy administration started a series of basic reforms and was preoccupied only by the leftists and Mossadegh's National Front. He sincerely thought that he had muzzled the mullahs once and for all. Thus, in 1976, he contended in an interview that the mullahs did not represent a threat as they "had lost the monopoly on education they enjoyed in the past." "I have some enemies: the communists, the Islamic Marxists and the like."[17] This illusion of the Shah served the purposes of Khomeini as the mullahs enjoyed relative freedom of action: the secret police concentrated its attention on the Mujahiddins (Islamic Marxists), the National Front, and the liberal elements of the intelligentsia.

This situation suited Khomeini fine since he was left almost totally free to pursue his hidden agenda. He was teaching his ideas to the young mullahs and multiplying the number of his devotees. He, as well as his minions, kept a low profile; nevertheless, the land reform forced him to break his apparent silence. The clergy opposed the reform, because it would cut their profits from the revenues of vast estates bequeathed by rich people to a kind of charitable foundation managed by the clergy (*owghaf*). Boroujerdi, despite his good relations with the Shah's government, had opposed a previous land reform proposal that was modest and extremely limited in scope compared to the one voted on in 1963. In March of that year, Khomeini all of a sudden unlimbered his guns and called the believers to protest against the land reform and other measures. Demonstrations and counter-demonstrations in the streets of Qum resulted in some casualties. Despite all the efforts of his followers, Khomeini's appeal failed to mobilize the masses, however, it infuriated the Shah, whose authoritarian disposition had already taken shape. The monarch performed a pilgrimage to Qum where he delivered an acerbic speech against the mullahs whom he dubbed as "black" reactionaries (the communists being in his vocabulary the "red" reactionaries). Almost immediately Khomeini paid him back in his own coin: in his *Faizieh* seminar, he compared the Shah to the Ummayad usurpers who had assassinated the Prophet's grandchild Hussein in the Kerbela desert (seventh century) and accused the sovereign of connivance with Israel. The ayatollah concluded his diatribe with the slogan "Islam is in danger."

Upon his return to Tehran, the Shah ordered Khomeini's arrest. After a few weeks in prison, he was confined in a villa under house arrest. Finally, the monarch allowed him to return to Qum and even resume his teaching. In the Iranian context, the Shah's leniency was interpreted as a sign of weakness by the public and of stark defeat by Khomeini's followers. At any rate, with his medieval mind-set and his belief in his own rightness and the protection of Allah and the Saint Imams, Khomeini did not consider himself defeated. On the contrary, he was convinced that the Shah had yielded! In his way of thinking, the whole episode was nothing but a *trial* imposed on him by the Almighty in order to evaluate his ability to represent the 12th (Hidden) Imam on earth. He took advantage of the respite to instruct his inner circle on the necessity of starting preparations for the final confrontation with the enemies of Islam in general and the Shah in particular. His followers resuscitated the *Fedayin-e-Islam* under a new and less aggressive appellation, the Hojatich society, which today devotes most of its energy to converting Bahais.

In 1964, Khomeini faced two supplementary tests. First, two of his followers who had organized demonstrations in Tehran were condemned to death and executed. Second, his diatribes did not succeed in provoking new public protests against the reforms. Changing tactics, he called on believers to assemble in Qum's streets to hear his message. He spoke to them from his house through a number of microphones suspended on the electric line poles. The gist of his statement was that the United States and Israel were conspiring with the Shah in order to erase Islam; only the mullahs and their leaders could, with the help of believers, thwart this satanic scheme. After that, Khomeini invited the other ayatollahs to join him in denouncing the reforms as anti-Islamic. They agreed, but their opposition was expressed in very moderate terms.

The Shah reacted by ordering Khomeini's exile instead of letting him be condemned to death by a military tribunal for fomenting sedition. Again, the Shah appeared weak, but the masses were not in the mood to follow the appeal of a low-ranking ayatollah. Khomeini, after a short stay in Turkey, went to Najaf where he enjoyed more freedom of action because of Iraq's enmity toward Iran.

Thus ended the first round of the fight between the Shah and Khomeini. The former considered himself victorious while the latter did not admit defeat.

DREAMS OF GRANDEUR

By the mid-1960s, the Shah seemed to succeed in all his undertakings: he had just gotten rid of Khomeini, his internal and most dangerous nemesis; the Soviet Union ceased to attack him and opted for a good neighborly policy; his reform programs were bearing their first fruits; many educated people who had been reluctant to cooperate with the reform programs were now in the government or the development agencies; the liberal opposition was losing steam; and the clergy was calming down.

But the Shah's character underwent a gradual change between 1965 and 1975. Hubris seized him and he came to consider himself superior to everybody inside and outside the country. He ceased listening to his aides. His dreams of grandeur overbalanced his sense of reality. The oil boom of the 1970s accentuated these negative traits and megalomania overtook him completely. Very quickly his arrogance became limitless. He used to stay long hours alone in his office refusing to see anybody, woolgathering about the future. He would come out of these solitary thinking bouts with extravagant new programs that nobody dared to question. He had identified himself with his father, about whom he had once told an interviewer: "Not only the state officials but I myself held him in such high respect that none of us would ever dream of discussing with him in the sense of a give-and-take argument. I could only express my views and drop hints; any discussion was out of the question."[18] And he explained in these words his conception of kingship: "A king in Iran represents the people. ... He is the teacher, the master, the father, he is everything."[19]

He renamed the White Revolution: Revolution of the Shah and the People. And he emerged from one of his solitary meditations with the idea of *The Great Civilization*, a book which was published a year before the Islamic revolution. He developed in it his dream of transforming Iran into "one of the five great industrial powers of the world" before the end of the twentieth century. He ordered that the book become the "Bible" of the *one party* he created at the end of 1976 to replace all other tolerated political groups. "Monarchy," he asserted, "is the powerful underpin of the Great Civilization and at the same time the guardian of all its values and moral and material achievements."[20]

More and more he referred in his speeches and interviews to the Aryan ancestors of Persians. Thus, to cite only one instance, he declared in 1977 to an Indian journalist, "Iran never lost its ethos. Despite setbacks, reverses, even national calamities, the legacy of Cyrus, this flaming Aryan torch of ours, has been kept alight and passed on through our history, from generation to generation, linking the past to the present and insuring the future."[21] In 1971, he had already celebrated in a grandiose pageant the 2500th anniversary of the founding of the Persian Empire by Cyrus. In this regard, he told the Indian journalist, "Our White Revolution not only has its source but finds many parallels in the enlightened rule of Cyrus the Great. The Persepolis celebrations signified the reawakening of national pride in our rich heritage, coupled with the confidence of achievements deriving from our recent successes. This provided our people with the stimulus to identify themselves with their ancient land and its traditional monarchy."[22] On the Persepolis extravaganza, he affirmed, "Time, world and history then seemed to meet in Persepolis."

With the sudden tripling of oil prices and the multiplication of development programs, corruption swelled in the higher strata of society and especially among the members of the royal family, but the Shah was weak in his relations with his sisters and brothers and let them get into all sorts of shaky and scandalous business. Lost in his dreams of grandeur, he failed to understand the mounting concept of human rights and the expanding role of nongovernmental organizations such as Amnesty International. He also failed to appreciate the causes and effects of the late 1960s student revolt in Europe and the United States and its influence on Iranian students both inside and outside Iran. He underestimated the urban guerrilla and terrorist movements that were developing not only in

Iran, but also in the region and elsewhere. Finally, he seemed to ignore the consequences of détente of the cold war, which had brought him the American government's unconditional support. The Carter administration that entered the White House in 1977 considered him as a rather cumbersome ally and looked forward to a change in Iran's political system.[23]

THE VINDICTIVE AYATOLLAH

During all that period, Khomeini was organizing his forces. His disciples as well as his former students, on the pretext of pilgrimages to holy Shiite sites in Iraq, visited him regularly and brought back to Iran his instructions to his followers. Obviously the Iranian secret police could not watch him in Iraq as closely as in Qum. Khomeini's entourage took advantage of this situation to establish close contacts with the leaders of the large Shiite community in southern Lebanon. A former student of Khomeini, Moussa Sadr, had established himself as a top religious and political guide there. In Lebanon, Khomeini's envoys met with some Iranian dissidents who had joined the ranks of the PLO (such as Chamran and Ghotbzadeh). Through them, they met with Arafat and his top aides, who agreed to train Iranians in their guerrilla camps.

In the meantime, leftists exiled in Europe had helped the Iranian students, whose numbers were rapidly swelling, to form a united front against the Shah, known as the Confederation of Iranian Students. Khomeini ordered Muslim students to actively cooperate with them. In the United States as well as in other Western countries, the Confederation alerted local student organizations, leftist and liberal political parties, and the media about repression in Iran. Amnesty International became particularly active. Writing clubs also protested against the Shah's regime. It was said at the time that communists and big oil companies were funding the Confederation. At any rate, the students seemed to enjoy important financial resources. The Confederation organized demonstrations everywhere in Europe and America against the Shah and his ministers who travelled outside the country. Intellectuals wrote pamphlets which were distributed everywhere. By 1977, the protests against the Iranian regime had become a constant and vocal annoyance for the Shah. The Muslim students were gaining high positions in the Confederation. The Mujahiddins, who called themselves Muslim Marxists, failed to mobilize the peasants and workers. Unsuccessful in the countryside, they transformed themselves into urban guerrillas and terrorist groups. They assassinated a number of American military advisers. In all these antiregime activities, the mullahs kept a low profile until the last stages of the overthrow of the regime, letting the secular dissidents occupy the forestage.

Like the Shah in Tehran, Khomeini, in Najaf, seemed removed from the realities of the world. He spent days in meditative retreat, refusing to see even his family and his closest aides. He dreamed about the particulars of his Islamic state. He thought about the ways and means to establish in Iran the kind of Islamic government the Prophet ran in the seventh century in Medina and Ali ran in Kufa in the eighth century. But what he called the true Islam resembled more what had overtaken the Muslim world in the twelfth century when almost at the same time and everywhere fundamentalist interpretations of the Koran had become the core of the religion.[24] Contrary to the Shah's, Khomeini's lifestyle had not changed. One can even say that it had become more ascetic than before! Opposed to the ostentation and luxuries of the Imperial Court in Tehran, the ayatollah conducted a simple, almost destitute mode of existence. But as a French proverb says, *"les extrêmes se touchent"* (extremes connect). Khomeini's so-called true Islamic government, as events were going to prove, was as fanciful and chimerical as the Shah's Great Civilization! Moreover, by considering himself as a descendant of the Prophet (*seyed*) and the representative of the 12th Imam (Hidden Imam), Khomeini was not so far from the Shah who, with the 1971 Persepolis festivities, had linked himself to Cyrus and the Achaemenian dynasty!

In any case, there is no dearth of common traits between the two men who nurtured profound hatred for each other. They had grandiose dreams of restoration: Khomeini wanted to recreate the Prophet and Ali's rules, the Shah, to reestablish Cyrus's empire; they both were obstinate and spiteful; they harbored extremely simplistic views about the problems of their country and the world; they believed in conspiracy theories; they did not admit contradiction; they thought they knew everything better than anybody else; they believed they were guided by God; they were inclined toward dictatorship. Khomeini once proclaimed: "From the religious standpoint I am entitled to act as I do.... When I beheld the magnitude of the revolutionary movement, I saw God's intervention in it.... It couldn't be the making of men...."[25] The Shah for his part affirmed: "Without Divine blessing, my revolution would have not been possible. Without God's support, I would have been a man like any other."[26] Once in power, Khomeini showed as much intolerance as his predecessor and exerted an even stricter authoritarianism and more cruel repression. Of the Marxists, the ayatollah said, "They are like children and know nothing about Iranian society."[27] The Shah said, "These persons (the Marxists), in their adulthood, act like children."[28] Curiously enough, the success of the Shah in 1963 and that of Khomeini in 1979 were both sealed by referendums which produced exactly the same amount of votes: over 95% in favor of monarchy and modernization (in the case of the Shah) and over 95% against monarchy and modernization (in the case of the ayatollah)!

Thus, the two men who nursed such hatred for each other and had different lifestyles, were nevertheless oddly alike, as if they were cast in the same mold. They were almost similar in their ideas of governance, yet, they contrasted in lifestyle and worldly appearance! How can one explain such a paradox?

The truth is that the resemblances between them can be traced in *all those who have governed Iran since the remotest past*; indeed, through history, Iranian sovereigns possess a number of common characteristics and traits. One can even affirm that without these characteristics they could not have ascended to the throne. It is as though some kind of invisible crucible exists in which all the candidates to the supreme leadership of the Iranian nation must spend a period of incubation in order to acquire the necessary qualities of Iranian governance and become acceptable to the people. In order to discover this crucible and to describe the characteristics of Iranian leadership, it is necessary to examine the history, and more specifically, the *mythology* of the Iranian nation.

CHAPTER TWO

The Enduring Mythology of Persia

Religious beliefs constitute the essence of spiritual life of every society, for without such a firm backing a society, however advanced it may be in respect to material comfort, will only lead a bewildered and aimless existence. True faith is the greatest guarantee of spiritual health and moral perseverance and the most powerful mainstay of every human being in facing life problems, great or small, and at the same time the surest moral guardian of every society.

Our people enjoy the blessing of living under the banner of the most progressive and elevated religious principles, namely those of the sacred faith of Islam. This faith, whose sublime teachings and principles embrace the most perfect material and spiritual advancement of mankind, can be the highest guide to individuals and to society at every stage of social evolution. The pride and the secret and the complete success of our revolution lie in this very fact that the principles of this revolution are throughout inspired by the spirit and essence of the exalted teachings of Islam.

Guess who wrote the above text, which implies the superiority of Islam over all other religions, rejects any separation of society and faith, and attributes to Islam the victory of the revolution? It certainly reminds one of Ayatollah Ruhollah Khomeini, who has developed such ideas in his books and interviews. The author could also be a lesser ayatollah or even any underling of Iran's present theocratic regime. Both Ayatollah Rafsanjani and President Khatami have uttered comparable notions at a Friday prayer or in political gatherings. At any rate, the ideas developed in the preceding quotation are spread, day and night, by the media of the Islamic Republic of Iran.

The extract is actually excerpted from a 1978 book composed by Muhammad Reza Pahlavi, the last Shah of Iran, under the title *Toward the Great Civilization!* Although the Shah was alluding to his White Revolution and reforms such as women's equal rights, which Khomeini promptly condemned in the name of his brand of Islam, nevertheless, when it comes to religion and spirituality, many passages of the monarch's and Khomeini's publications are interchangeable! This should not surprise the reader: as I have indicated in the previous chapter, both men possess quite a number of common traits. Contrary to Khomeini's accusations, the Shah was a believer and respected the Shiite Saints. The similitudes between Iranian leaders, as I pointed out in the preceding chapter, go back to the remotest past. Thus, Cyrus or Darius as well as any Sassanid emperor could have authored the quotation, provided one replaces in the text Islam with Zoroastrianism!

Continuity is the hallmark of Iranian culture. Indeed, many constants blaze the trails of the 3,000-year-old Iranian history. Present historians, as well as those of the past century, have often emphasized what they call the *permanence of Iran*, meaning that old Iranian traditions have survived the many calamities and invasions that have struck the Caspian Plateau.¹ Curiously enough, the *mind-set* of Iranians has barely changed over the centuries. Many ancient beliefs linger in the mind of Iranians today and sometimes trigger reactions which seem incomprehensible to foreign observers. I remember a French journalist friend of mine who, after a visit to Iran in 1981, asked me, "Are you Iranians insane? You stunned the whole world by overthrowing with your bare hands the powerful dictatorship of the Shah. And now your compatriots voluntarily, if not enthusiastically, submit to another dictator, even more totalitarian and repressive than the Shah and his regime!" No, Iranians are far from being mad; they are only prisoners of their own permanence, of their own mores. Despite its undeniable material and technical development, Iran, in 1978, remained at heart a *traditional society* in the sense given to that term by sociologists and historians.

The Shah, prey to his own hubris, entertained the illusion that Iran had already broken the walls of backwardness and underdevelopment and become part of the modern and advanced world. Despite his deep-seated anti-Marxist philosophy and his almost superstitious religious beliefs, material signs of progress dazzled him to a fault and blinded him to all other factors. For example, in his 1978 *Toward the Great Civilization*, he wrote,

> Tehran, which never appeared on the list of places in which worldwide economic activities occurred, became one of the most animated centers of the world for such activities. The Iranian industrial era started.... Between the beginning of the (White) Revolution and today (1977), the figure representing Gross National Product (GNP), at current prices, rose from 340 billion to 5,682 billion rials. In other words, the said production had increased more than 16-fold in the space of only 15 years. The volume of national savings, which is an index of the soundness of the state of the public economy, increased from 45 to 1,509 billion rials. The annual rate of

growth of our country's economy, which for many years has figured at the head of the international list as the highest rate of economic growth in the world, is at present 13.8%. Average per capita income, which was at the beginning of the Revolution 174 dollars, has reached 2,200 in the first half of the current year.... Our country which until 1973 did not figure among the twenty wealthy countries which form the subject of studies by the International Monetary Fund, has occupied since 1974 the 13th place among them....[2]

It is true that in a matter of only 15 years a whole economic and social infrastructure had been built up, the solidity of which was proven by the long and bloody war provoked by Iraq. Indeed, without such an infrastructure Iraq would have rapidly defeated Iran! Yet this modern and wealthy Iran, whose rapid emergence had bewildered world experts in the 1970s, was only the tip of an iceberg, of which two thirds was still steeped in the Middle Ages! But dazzled by the initial successes of the rapid economic progress and his obsessive dream of the Great Civilization, and also prodded by his terminal malady, the Shah could not or did not want to acknowledge reality in its entirety: Iran, despite its rapid and tangible progress, remained largely a traditional society. Despite the advice of his aides and some foreign experts, he decided to gallop through his programs.

IRAN: A "TRADITIONAL" SOCIETY

One characteristic of premodern or traditional societies is what specialists dub an archaic mind-set or premodern way of thinking, which prompts masses as well as elites to assume, among other things, that *uncontrollable forces* rule them.[3] This predisposition covers a vast gamut of beliefs starting with simple superstitions such as the evil eye and ending up with complicated elaborations like satanic plots by the great powers. Thus, Ayatollah Khomeini, like all other militant Muslim fundamentalists, Sunnite or Shiite (such as, for instance, Sheikh Yassin, the spiritual leader of the Palestinian Hamas extremist group), was *sincerely* convinced of the existence of a conspiracy by Israel and the West aiming to erase Islam from the surface of the planet. In the view of these militant fundamentalists, the Crusades never ended. They earnestly see Great Satans (and lesser ones) around them!

In the absence of a criterion helping to separate facts from fiction and reality from legend, people of traditional societies are forced to speculate, to imagine, and to fancy. They constantly sway from bewilderment to dread and vice versa. They resort to heaven and rely on God; they leave themselves to fate and destiny; whatever happens to them comes from outside, from uncontrollable forces; they see signs everywhere from the beyond; natural catastrophes are God's punishment imposed on men for their misconduct.[4] Conversely, good happenings or successes are considered as rewards from the Almighty. In 1979, many Iranians, even highly educated ones, pretended to have seen Khomeini's face on the full moon (an event which in the Iranians' belief "anoints" the person). In the same vein, the masses firmly believed that Allah inspired Khomeini's actions and destroyed the American helicopters which landed in the Tabass desert for rescuing the hostages! Spates of other examples can be cited.

One can say that Iranians (not unlike other Third World nations and sometimes groups of immigrants in the most advanced countries), tow with them, as it were, large chunks of medieval and even more remote concepts and beliefs. Indeed, many ancient Iranian legends remain alive in Iran and have also pervaded the Islamic,

Judaic, and Christian faiths. In this respect, some historians consider that the Jewish messiah, the return of Jesus, the Islamic Sunnite *Mahdi* and the Shiite Hidden Imam, originate in the Zoroastrian awaited Shoshyant. In any case, the masses firmly believe in occultism and reincarnation. Thus, at the start of the Islamic revolution, a number of Iranians among the most devout saw in Khomeini the reincarnation of the awaited 12th Imam. Moreover, as previously indicated, Khomeini himself affirmed that he had been mandated by God and would guide the country on behalf of the Hidden Imam. In ancient times, Darius, for his part, proclaimed that he was the reincarnation of the legendary hero Thraetaona (Feridun), who saved Iran from the clutches of the tyrant Zahak and his master Ahriman (the devil). Even today, in some parts of Iran, one finds people who believe that the Shah did not die and will return one day. I personally have seen in 1945, in Tehran, some highly educated people denying the death of Hitler and affirming that he went on hiding in a remote mountain!

Be this as it may, myths are alive in traditional societies and continue to determine individual and collective conduct. As Mircea Eliade reminded us in almost all his books, myths always recount a primordial event that happened at the beginnings of time. They describe, so to say, emergences of the sacred in the actual world, and awaken and orient humans' activities. By listening to a myth, men learn not only about the manner in which something came into existence, but also how they must themselves proceed in their lives.[5] (see, for instance, Eliade's *The Myth of the Eternal Return* and *Aspects du Mythe*).

According to ancient Iranian cosmology, every terrestrial phenomenon, whether abstract or concrete, corresponds to a celestial term or model.[6] In a way, it can be said that Iranians unconsciously repeat gestures and rituals initiated by other beings (their real or legendary ancestors) who were not ordinary men, but heroes or prophets. To confine my remarks to the case of Iran, I add that many primeval beliefs have survived and continue to permeate the present. Pre-Islamic mythology and the legends concerning Prophet Muhammad and the 12 Imams are all kept alive through education and oral recitation by public storytellers.

More than that, Iranians have always been attracted by their long and glorious past. Travelling inside Iran in the 1860s, the French writer and diplomat Count de Gobineau noted:

> [The Persians] are a very ancient nation and as they themselves say probably the oldest nation which had had a regular government and functioned as a great people on earth. This truth is present in the mind of the whole Iranian family. It is not only the educated class that knows and expresses it; the lowest people too are proud of it, repeat it and often discuss it. Here one finds the basis of their firm feeling of superiority as well as a large part of their moral heritage.... Tradition exerts a great authority on the mind of the population.... The past is even a favorite subject of conversation among the populace ... The Persian nationality evinces itself by one additional symptom: the affection at the remembrance of the Imams. The latter are the sons and grandsons of Ali who himself is included in this veneration which verges on real adoration. There is no Persian who does not feel a profound attachment for these saint persons; and whatever your counterpart's intimate beliefs, even if his opinions were a far cry from Muslim's faith, he would not accept that one speaks lightly about the Imams...."[7]

In an environment in which no clear separation exists between natural and supernatural, and between possible and impossible happenings, historic events can easily be, so to say, *mythified*. In this perspective, for instance, the death of Hussein (son of Ali and grandson of Prophet Muhammad), besieged by the Ummayad general Yazid in the Kerbela desert, was linked to ancient Iranian pre-Islamic mourning rituals of heroes.[8] These rituals, repeated every year, have become a basic manifestation of Shiite faith even in Arab areas.[9] Likewise, as demonstrated by Mircea Eliade, natural catastrophies and death can be valued in a positive way and therefore accepted by society.[10] Thus, the Iraqis were bewildered by the numerous Iranian suicidal martyrs who during the eight years of war walked before the tanks and the foot soldiers in the mine fields. According to Shiite mythology, the imitation of the fate of Hussein, the Prince of Martyrs, instantly opens the gates of paradise.

I do not intend, in the limited space of this book, to take stock of all the vast and extremely rich Iranian mythology. I would instead concentrate on a few elements of the ancient legends that might shed light on some unexplained aspects of the 1978–79 Iranian revolution. One such element can be found in the story of *Jamshid and Zahak*, which is widespread among Iranians of all classes.

JAMSHID AND ZAHAK

According to that legend, there was a time when Ahura Mazda (God in the Zoroastrian religion), upset by humans' greedy and sinful behavior, withdrew light from earth and in the ensuing darkness our planet became the realm of Ahriman (the devil in Zoroastrianism), who supported tyrants. Then, one day, Jamshid ascended to the throne and started a rule of justice and progress. Ahura Mazda, pleased by his behavior and deeds, returned the light, thus forcing Ahriman, the Prince of Darkness, to flee the earth. Jamshid could therefore reconstruct the country. He built

Persepolis (in Persian, Throne of Jamshid); he set up a system of irrigation that revived arid lands; he constructed roads that linked the cities and favored trade; he helped peasants and artisans. During a great part of Jamshid's reign, people enjoyed a healthy and comfortable life, and the whole globe thrived under his reign. But, in the end, the monarch believed that his subjects' well-being and happiness proceeded from himself alone. Overwhelmed by hubris and conceit, he forgot his indebtness to Ahura Mazda. He assembled the people and told them: "I have given you all this wealth and comfort. You should therefore worship me as your king and the master of the world." Disappointed by these words, Ahura Mazda once again withdrew light and as a result all the earthly splendor faded away and the tongues of the people grew bold against Jamshid. Ahriman returned and helped Zahak to overthrow Jamshid and take his place. In order to prevent any good deed on the part of the new king and to ensure continuous tyranny, he kissed Zahak on his naked shoulders from which two black serpents sprang up. He told Zahak, "You must feed them daily the brains of young adolescents. Otherwise they will bite you." A reign of terror started. People lamented and prayed for Ahura Mazda to send them a savior.

The parallel of this story with the events of the 1970s is remarkable. The program of reforms that started in 1963 was just beginning to yield its first fruits when the Shah, falling, as it were, into the sin of presumption, ordered the famous Persepolis festival of September 1971 to commemorate the 2500th anniversary of the foundation of the Iranian Empire by Cyrus and to present himself as the heir and continuator of the great Achaemenian king. After the tripling of oil prices in 1974–75, his arrogance became limitless. He adopted a teaching tone and in all his interviews gave lessons to the leaders of the world, including those of the well-developed countries, and more particularly the superpowers!

To come back to the Jamshid and Zahak legend, the people, as already indicated, suffering from the tyranny of the new monarch, were lamenting and praying for Ahura Mazda to send a savior who would deliver them from the clutches of the bloody tyrant who killed two adolescents every day in order to feed the serpents on his shoulder. Pitying the wretched citizens, Ahura Mazda inspired the blacksmith Kaveh to bring back from the peak of Damavand the hero Feridun and start a revolt against Zahak, who was eventually dethroned.

Khomeini and his underlings seemed to follow the same mythological cycle even more quickly than the Shah did. Indeed, in less time than the monarch, they turned into unrelenting tyrants. It is of no importance that Khomeini and Khamenei relate themselves to Imam Ali rather than to Cyrus, as the Shah used to do. What is striking is that Iranian leaders, as far back as history and legend go, have always become despots if they were not already when they came to power! They seem to reproduce the Indian mythological diptych of Mitra–Viruna (the benevolent and violent aspects of the ruler). The late French scholar Georges Dumézil has found the same double feature of sovereignty among Iranians, Germans, Celts, and other Indo-European peoples.[11] Each nation's particular circumstances and history have wrought modifications and woven local features into their legends. In the case of Iranians, it seems that the duality is confined in one person. But it manifests itself at different moments, so that the people are always fobbed. Indeed, Iranian leaders remind one of Stevenson's Jekyll and Hyde!

THE ROSTAM SYNDROME

The Iranian leader is in fact a kind of two-faced father: compassionate on the one hand, but also, and more often than not, stern and even cruel. He is the "father of the nation" and therefore is supposed to provide for the well-being of his citizens-children; but at the same time he is a very strict and adamant father who goes as far as putting them to death if they disobey him. He protects them as long as they submit to his commands, but does not hesitate to punish them severely when they fail to carry out his orders. Iran's history bears witness to numerous kings who massacred or blinded members of their own family or entourage as well as whole groups of citizens. Replacing the shahs, the mullahs followed suit. Thus Khomeini did not hesitate to confirm the death sentence against Ghotbzadeh who had helped him climb to power and stood at his side in exile like a son. Bani Sadr, the first president of the Islamic Republic, whom Khomeini considered as his spiritual son, had to flee in order to escape the fate of Ghotbzadeh! Like the Shah before them, the mullahs execute daily droves of so-called drug traffickers and other offenders.

The despotic nature of Iranian rulers can be traced to several characters in the ancient mythological tales and particularly to the great champion Rostam. This legendary superhero, was resuscitated by Ferdowsi in his monumental epic poem, *Shahnameh* (Book of Kings), written toward the end of the tenth century. From early childhood, all Iranians know his story as told to them by their mothers or nannies. Storytellers constantly recite the exploits of the Iranian superman in teahouses or other public places. As the French philosopher and orientalist Henry Corbin once remarked, Ferdowsi's *Shahnameh* is tantamount to an Iranian Bible:

It perpetuates the heroic exploits and doings of the nation's ancient times.

Among the many strands of thematic interest going on all at
once in the poem, one of the most important concerns the ongoing battles between Iran, a country of sedentary culture and thriving cities, and Touran, a land of steppes and nomadism. Two other
recurrent themes are the laments about martyred heroes and the
descriptions of sunrise, which reflect, in my opinion, two important psychological traits of Iranians: propensity toward exaggerated mourning and sorrow on the one hand, and a deep sense of
Iran's historical fate of a succession of defeats and dismember-
ments followed by stunning restorations. After each quirk of destiny, a savior king appears, who reestablishes independence, starts
a new dynasty, and reimposes the national culture and mores.
These successive ups and downs reflect events happening in
heaven, where Ahura Mazda (God in Zoroastrianism) and his angels constantly repel Ahriman's (Satan's) attacks.

Another repetitive theme in Ferdowsi's epic is that of father-son
and king-champion conflicts. Professor Dick Davis has recently
noted that the tension between fathers and sons "becomes particularly noticeable in the story of Esfandyar (arguably the climactic
tale of the entire *Shahnameh*) as the *necessity of obedience to
monarch and father* has become *religiously locked* into the society's
ethos by the advent of Zoroastrianism which, at least as it is presented in the *Shahnameh*, insisted on the absolute obedience of a
son to his father, and of a subject to his king."[12] In this respect Rostam occupies a large role in the poem. He is probably the most
well-known legendary hero, a kind of unbeatable superman.

One day Rostam goes hunting near the border of Touran. After
eating lunch, he takes a nap. On waking he finds that his horse has

disappeared. He walks into the kingdom of Samangan and is invited to be a guest of the king. He spends the night with Tahmineh, the daughter of the king, and, after he recovers his horse, returns home. Nine months later, his son Sohrab is born and grows rapidly to become a strong and mighty warrior in the Touranian armies. He constantly searches for his father, whom he has never met. During a war, he is pitted against Rostam and brings him to heel in that first encounter. But in a second confrontation Rostam wounds him fatally before discovering his real identity. The superman gives vent to his profound sorrow. Yet the dying son consoles the grieving father by telling him, "You must not weep.... What happened is what had to happen."

Be this as it may, the story of Rostam strikes one as a total reverse of the Greek legend of Oedipus, who inadvertently kills his own father. I was attending a seminar on psychoanalysis in Paris, in the mid-1950s, when I questioned the universality of Freud's Oedipus complex. It then appeared to me that in the Iranian tradition sons do not kill their fathers and are often slain by them; they have to await his natural or accidental exit before taking his place. Reflecting on the events of 1978–79 that culminated with the ascent to power of Ayatollah Khomeini, one should not forget that when the Shah left Iran on January 16, 1979, he was still the monarch (a weakened one, to be sure; but nevertheless, a sovereign). He therefore was not overthrown in the literal sense of the term. Moreover, in 1978, the demonstrators in the streets never walked toward his palace as would have been natural in a revolution.[13] Khomeini came back from exile *only after the Shah's departure.* A similar script presided over the change of dynasty in 1925. Reza Khan, then prime minister, persuaded Ahmad Shah Qajar to leave the country on vacation before he endeavored to replace him on the Peacock throne.

The power of tradition in Iran is such that Khomeini himself, while pretending to act in the name of Islam and on behalf of the Hidden Imam, followed step by step the pre-Islamic model. Indeed, when invited in 1978 to return to Qum with international guarantees of security and freedom of speech and action, he refused and demanded that, first, the Shah leave Iran on vacation! Consciously or not, he knew all too well that by accepting the proposed arrangement he would put himself in the position of a son (the Shah remaining the father of the nation) and could not achieve his goal of an Islamic republic. But as soon as he became the father-ruler in February of 1979, he demanded the immediate return of the ex-monarch who in the meantime had become a son whom Khomeini wanted to recover in order to punish!

I have chosen to call this Iranian pattern in the father-son relationship the *Rostam Syndrome*, after the mythological legend of Rostam and Sohrab. It is true that all traditional societies, and especially the Third World countries, possess some sort of paternalistic structure. But in most of them, traditions somehow limit the absolutism of the patriarch. Although the latter's decision is final, he often consults his sons grouped in councils. Even God in the Bible and the Koran relieves Abraham of the obligation to sacrifice his son. In Iranian tradition, paternalism is not only authoritarian and absolute, it is also despotic. This type of father-son relationship pervades Iranian society at all levels. The Rostam Syndrome exerts its deep influence from the top to the bottom of the social pyramid. Every father is the sole master in his domain (country or simple household). Every tribal chief or landowner is the absolute ruler of his territory. The high priest has the last word in his priesthood: Grand ayatollahs, for instance, are dubbed "source of imitation," meaning that the faithful must do as they say. The political leader enjoys absolute power. The feudal landlord has full authority over his peasants (including the right to put them to death!). The ordinary father imposes his own law at home.

Thus, we find at each social level a "father" who becomes a "son" in relation to the upper levels. As a result, plain citizens are in a way eternal children who always remain in the custody of a father. Up to 1979, the Shah was the supreme father. As Muhammad Reza Pahlavi wrote in his last book: "The king in Iran is a teacher, a master, a father; in short he is everything."[14] In the same vein, Khomeini calls his theory of governance *Velayate Faghih* (Guardianship of the Theologian): in the view of ayatollahs, Iranians are children in need of a custodian!

Thus, invisible bonds of servitude link all levels of Iranian society from roots to branches. The supreme ruler himself, in a way, is far from being completely free, since ultimately, he must submit to God's authority. In the first pages of this chapter, I evoked the question of a French friend returning from a 1980 visit to Iran: "Are Iranians mad?" The answer is obviously negative. Indeed, Iranians abandoned the Shah only when he lost his "fathership," by becoming weak and fleeing the country, and when they found a replacement in the person of Khomeini. Screaming the slogan of "Islam is in danger," the latter startled them and appeared to them with the aura of a savior sent by God. In February of 1979 his plane landed in Mehrabad's airport: he literally alighted from heaven!

Obviously, democracy cannot take root and grow in such a paternalistic and despotic environment. I remember my perplexity in history courses when I was attending high school. Why did Persians and Greeks who both were Indo-European cousins wage constant wars against each other? The explanations of my professors as well as those of historians referring to the character of the rulers and to economic arguments about trade routes and other features (such as exiled politicians of both sides) never totally convinced me. Now it seems clear to me that the systems of governance of the two nations constituted a permanent danger for each other. If the stern father rule spilled into Greek cities it would endanger democracy and vice versa. Today in the Middle East we witness something of that kind. Behind the bickerings and wars, mythologies and political systems loom large. For one thing, Israel's democracy constitutes a constant danger for the Muslim authoritarian governments and vice versa. At any rate, after several centuries of Greek interlude, Persians found nothing better than to reestablish their ancestral totalitarian political structures with the Sassanid empire which collapsed a couple of centuries later under the assault of Arabia's Muslim Bedouins.

In this perspective and coming back to the events that ended the Iranian monarchy and replaced it with Khomeini's Islamic authoritarian rule, one should remember that by 1977, under the pressure of the Carter administration, Muhammad Reza Shah, already deeply impressed by Juan Carlos's example in Spain, wanted to liberalize his regime. He envisioned installing a real constitutional monarchy, authorizing all political parties, and organizing free elections, under international scrutiny, in June 1979.[15] This new trend in his reforms, much more than the modernization inaugurated with the White Revolution, constituted a direct threat to the influence of the Shiite clergy whose paternalistic structure could only tolerate (and thrive under) the despotic father-rule of the traditional system. Learning about the Shah's intentions, Khomeini, who had already locked horns with him on several occasions in the 1950s and 1960s, acted immediately and fobbed both Iranian and Western liberals and secularists with his early "democratic" language.[16] As soon as he arrived in Iran after the departure of the Shah, he unlimbered his guns and put in place his absolutist medieval theocracy.

Be this as it may, one should constantly keep in mind the eminent place of the father in order to understand the unfolding of events in Iranian society of the past as well as the present. The Iranian father is not a symbolic figure, a father figure (like General de Gaulle or Chancellor Adenauer were in France and in Germany after World War II). To the contrary, he considers himself a *real father*, as clearly expounded in the forementioned quote from Muhammad Reza Shah's book. The same can be said of the ayatollahs and Imams. Shah, Imam, or simple head of an ordinary family, the Iranian father possesses an *absolute power* over his children in his particular realm. He is invested with limitless power by God or by tradition and he exerts it with the utmost harshness and severity. Nothing stops him in wielding it. In a way, he is an atavistic killer, as if he were seeking revenge for all he had suffered as a child before acceding to fathership. He recites the Koranic formula "In the name of God, the compassionate, the merciful" without paying attention to its real meaning. He is much more interested by the description of God's punishments than by that of the delights of paradise. When he is not wielding the sword, he handles the whip. Children, believers, and subjects must submit to the will of the father: head of family, ayatollah, or king. Furthermore, the Iranian must be ready to sacrifice his life if and when the circumstances demand it. Martyrdom pleases Allah and automatically opens the gates of Eden.

Clearly, the dread of the father is not fictional. Iranian history abounds in bloody episodes in which fathers literally kill their children and subjects. Since its inception, Iranian society has been based on a blanket delegation of limitless power to the father and on a total submission of the children. The Shah in the past and the ayatollahs today turn up their noses at the protests based on the Universal Declaration of Human Rights which they consider as contrary to many teachings of Allah's laws as edicted by the Koran or interpreted by the Islamic jurisprudents. In their views it threatens both Muslim and traditional Iranian identity.

What confused outside observers as well as some Iranians about the Islamic revolution is that, save for a limited group of intellectuals and educated members of society, the bulk of the Iranian citizens were not yearning for freedom, but rather looking for another father. The Shah with his so-called liberalizing program was softening his repressive rule. Under pressure by the United States and nongovernmental human rights organizations (such as Amnesty International) he pardoned some of his enemies (including Rajavi, the head of the Mujahiddins who had been condemned to death). In 1978, he did not react harshly against his opponents and, to the contrary, accepted all their demands. He showed weakness and therefore ceased to be a true father in the traditional sense.

The complexities of modern societies which were stealthily inching into the country with the reforms of the White Revolution, frightened the masses still accustomed to the simplicity and efficacy of traditional ways. Khomeini, aware of the dismay of the ordinary citizen in the face of change, used to a maximum pitch their creeping fears. For instance, he repeatedly criticized the civil courts that had taken over from clerics the dispensation of justice. He would say in this respect that it would take a civil court sometimes several years before ending a case and pronouncing a verdict, while Islamic tribunals would decide in two or three days.

In more general terms, he used to affirm:

> If a government applied Islamic criminal law during one single year, it would uproot all injustices and immoralities. Crimes should be punished by the Talion [law of retaliation]: sever the hand of a thief, put to death a murderer instead of imprisoning him, whip the adulterous. So-called humanitarian scruples are rather childish. According to Koranic law, any person filling up the seven conditions [being male, pubescent, believer, cognizant of Islamic law, fair; and not illegitimate or amnesiac] is habilitated to be judge in any law-case. He can thus judge in one day twenty different cases while Western justice takes years to tackle only one of them.[17]

He contended that all the reforms introduced by the so-called White Revolution were nothing but "westoxication!"

Such simple language was indeed soothing to the masses, bewildered by the sudden erruption of spates of novelties in their traditional environment. The Shah, who was acting like foreigners and speaking a complicated language, ceased to be a father to them. They felt like orphan children in need of a protector, of a custodian. They feverishly looked for a real father. And the new father revealed himself in the person of Khomeini, whose religious aura compensated for his frailty: he possessed the title of Imam and had proven his endurance and force in past battles against the Shah. One day he descended from heaven in a Boeing 747 and appeared to the throngs in the full light of noon's sunshine. Order was restored, as a new shah, a high-ranking religious one to boot, came to sit on the throne vacated by his runaway predecessor. The social pyramid, far from crumbling down, was rather reinforced. We touch here upon another aspect of Iranian mythology which might help us in clarifying some remaining riddles of the 1979 Islamic revolution, namely the tripartite concept of government and society.

THE THREE FUNCTIONS AND THE FOUR CLASSES

In this respect, I refer to the lifelong work of the French historian and linguist Georges Dumézil on Indo-European people. His research in the field of mythologies of the people of India, Persia, Caucasus, Scandinavia, and some other nations brought to light what he called the *tripartite ideology* in the structures and socioreligious organization as well as the imagination of the Indo-Europeans. This ideology implies the division of society into three superposed zones corresponding to three functions which are interdependent although not equally dignified: sovereignty, physical power, and prosperity. The first function itself is divided into two parts: political and religious leadership. Society can thrive only through the harmonious collaboration of the three hierarchical functions. This conception of governance can be visualized in the form of a pyramid: at the top one finds the two-headed sovereign power of king and high priest; immediately under this level, comes martial force (warriors); and then, prosperity, which encompasses agriculture, industry, trade, arts, and so on.

It is true that any human society comes to consider these three functions as vital when it organizes itself. But, as Dumézil showed, the Indo-Europeans, unlike others, built it into an explicit theory of governance. As for Iran, a description of a slightly modified version of this theory can be found in the letter of the Grand Priest Tanzar to the king of Tabaristan.[18] At the time of the first Sassanid monarchs, Tanzar was in charge of restoring the Mazdean faith and recuperating the sacred texts of the Avesta. The king of Tabaristan, a vassal of the Persian rulers, had asked Tanzar for some clarifications. In his answer the Iranian grand priest drew the attention of his correspondent to the fact that, according to religion, men are divided into four classes. This fact, he went on, is clearly stated in the sacred books and therefore cannot be contested or modified. At the very top is the *Shahinshah* (King of kings). Then comes the clergy, followed by the warriors; then the scribes and secretaries, including physicians, astronomers, and poets; finally those who perform the necessary services, including traders, peasants, and all other professionals. Tanzar continued his letter by insisting that this partition of functions guarantees order and security. He added that the passage from one category to another is forbidden, save for those individuals who show special talents. In their case, a request is submitted to the king and an inquest conducted by the clergy to confirm the special abilities of these individuals; then they would be authorized to join another class. Tanzar evoked a period during which corruption destroyed this structure and people grabbed ranks outside of their rights and aptitudes, causing the whole nation to fall prey to violence and disorder. Religion and well-being faded away until the wise *Shahinshah* (the first Sassanid ruler) reconstituted the dismembered body and put back each subject in his right caste and forbade transferences from one level to another.[19] At the end of his letter Tanzar alludes to a complaint by the king of Tabaristan about the excessive severity of the Sassanid rulers. The grand priest responds by stating that in the remote past *Shahinshahs* were less adamant because the people knew their place and respected the orders of the kings and of the religious class. After the corruption that engulfed the empire, the honor of the nation could not be restored without bloodshed and utmost severity in the implementation of laws.

The version of Tanzar's letter, which has survived, is an Arabic adaptation; it even contains a quote from the Koran (which obviously appeared two centuries later). The "four classes" instead of the "three functions" is also a distortion committed by the translators from Persian into Arabic. Notwithstanding these shortcomings, the letter remains a precious source of information about the tripartite ideology both in the pre-Islamic and post-Islamic periods. It underscores the survival of Iranian particularisms after the Arab onslaught; in short, the new rulers and the new religion could not expunge the old Persian mythology.

The tripartite ideology can help in understanding an intriguing event during the turmoil that preceded the Shah's fall: the almost total neutrality of the armed forces in the last months of the imperial regime. The monarchists affirm that the Shah was against bloodshed and therefore ordered the armed forces to stay put. But what about his generals as individuals? His own father, Reza Khan, who was a colonel and commanded the cossack brigade, participated in the 1921 coup! The generals who were pampered by the Shah could have stopped the demonstrations in a matter of hours. It was also in their personal interest to save their commander in chief and his regime. Many among them knew that they would later be executed by Khomeini. Why did they not budge? (Only a handful of members of the Imperial Guard acted at one point.) The followers of Khomeini pretend that the soldiers were good Muslims and therefore did not want to oppose the ayatollah. But even in the 1960s when the soldiers did not enjoy any special material advantage, the army did not hesitate to bring down the insurrection of the tribes or turn against Khomeini. In fact, the reason for the army's neutrality should be sought elsewhere. It is due to the very function of the army which, according to the tripartite ideology, is to make war or defend the country against aggression, not to insure internal security and order (responsibility of the police). In the case of the tribes' separatist movement, the soldiers acted because the integrity of the national territory was in jeopardy. The army, which had remained calm and neutral during the revolution, fought the Iraqi invaders with the utmost energy a year later! This was the function assigned to it by the tripartite ideology; indeed, while performing its duty of defense of the country, the army remained aloof in relation to other objectives of the Islamic government. It never participated in Khomeini's moves to export the Islamic revolution to other countries of the region. During the war with Iraq, at the start of the victorious counterattack that forced Saddam's soldiers to withdraw from the southern province of Khuzistan, General Zahirnejad, the commander of the operation, declared in answer to the question of a journalist, "The army will fight until the total liberation of the national territory." When another journalist asked him about Khomeini's slogan of "continuing the march toward Jerusalem," the general said without any hesitation, "This is a governmental affair and has nothing to do with the army."

The traditional neutrality of the Iranian army, stemming from deeply rooted mythological tradition, is indeed the reason why Iranian monarchs leaned on their own Imperial Guards for security. It is also why Khomeini created the Revolutionary Guards (*Pasdaran*) next to the regular army. Thus the neutrality of the regular army goes back very far in the past and conforms to the tripartite ideology. It is true that a member of the military (second level of the pyramid) might climb into the first level under certain conditions and circumstances. In order to do this, he must follow tests which confirm his talents for a higher level job or prove his ability by his behavior and actions. Thus, for instance, Reza Khan, before becoming Reza Shah, was coopted as minister of war by the

Prime Minister *Seyed* Zia-o-din whom he replaced a few months later! The seizure of the supreme power by Khomeini also took place in the framework of the tripartite ideology. Indeed, if the Sassanians placed the Shahinshah above everybody, nevertheless they had the Grand Priest (*Mobede-Mobedan*) stand at his side on the top level of the social pyramid. Khomeini's theory of *Velayate Faghih* (Custody of the Theologian) expels the secular authority from the top level at the behest of the religious one! It seems in accord with an Indian tradition in which the two aspects of sovereignty are united. Therefore, it can be said that Khomeini's theory leans on pre-Islamic traditions. This link with old Iranian mythology might explain the easy way in which the Islamic government was accepted not only by the masses but also by some more modern elements such as the members of the National Front (such as Bazargan and Sanjabi).

In this perspective the Islamic revolution appears as a kind of palace revolution. Indeed, it took place at the top level of the trifunctional pyramid, the palace, in which the Shah and the religious leader stood! To limit ourselves to the twentieth century, we see that Khomeini's upheaval followed the pattern of a number of other palace revolutions: the coronation of Reza Shah in 1925 with the blessing of the clergy; Reza Shah's abdication and his replacement by his son Muhammad Reza in 1941; the overthrow of Prime Minister Mossadegh and the return of the Shah in 1953; and the dismissal of feudal landowners and clergy members by Muhammad Reza Shah in 1963 (arrest and exile of Khomeini). Even in the 1905 constitutional revolution, one can find elements of a palace revolution as suggested by the tripartite ideology: it pitted feudal landowners and high clergy against the absolutism of the Qajar shahs.

It might be objected that the Islamic revolution, like some of its predecessors, was characterized by large popular demonstrations. But, actually, these demonstrations by the lower (third) level of the pyramid, square perfectly with Iranian tradition. The mythological order of Iranian society accounts for them, inasmuch as this behavior stems from the eminent place accorded to the father: whenever he disappears or weakens, the children (plain citizens) take to the streets. In the legend of Jamshid and Zahak, Kaveh the blacksmith called on the people to air their dissent. But before doing so, he went to Zahak's palace and defied him publicly, and the tyrant did not punish him. Here the legend seems incomplete, but at any rate, Kaveh left the king's court unharmed. This constituted a sign of Zahak's weakening authority; he lost his father-ruler features, he was not anymore the father-tyrant, and the fatherless people took to the streets (as Iranians did toward the end of 1978). Then, Kaveh went toward the Damavand mountain in order to bring back the new father, Feridun, intimated by Ahura Mazda. Feridun proved his aptitude to fathership and kingship by defeating Zahak and chaining him to the mountain. This action legitimized him; then the new father-king sent everybody back to their assigned places in the societal pyramid.

In a couple of months, Khomeini put an end to all street demonstrations which were not organized by his religious underlings. Everybody went back, so to say, to their natural places: the people to their third level of the pyramid; the opponants to prison or to exile in foreign countries. Given the present disorder and turmoil, as well as the bickering and struggle for power among the religious people, one can predict that the replacement of the mullah rule will also probably take the appearance of a palace revolution with a change at the top level of the pyramid (hopefully, replacement of the religious element by a secular one). Save for the Mujahiddins operating from Iraqi territory, no opposition group is recruiting soldiers. The only element that distinguishes the Islamic revolution from preceding ones lay in the unification of the two aspects of sovereignty into one ruler. Can one predict that such a unification would put an end to the competition between religious and secular leadership? It seems that this kind of tension, far from subsiding, is rather gaining momentum, as inside the clergy itself the *Velayate Faghih* theory is questioned.

Iran's events should be also considered in another framework: the conflict between traditionalists and modernizers which was fired up by the contacts with the West in the nineteenth century.

THE TWELFTH CENTURY AGAINST THE TWENTIETH

The origin of this conflict, which is common to all Muslim nations, can be traced to the twelfth century when, for a host of reasons, fundamentalist interpretations of the Koran triumphed first in the eastern part of the Muslim world (Arabia, Iran, Syria, Mesopotamia, Egypt) and later in the Western reaches of the Empire (North Africa, Andalusia). Under the fallacious pretext of submitting to God's will, Muslims, abetted by their religious and secular leaders, started to reject and then destroy the knowledge amassed by their scholars during the previous centuries.[20] What happened was tantamount to a collective "cultural suicide."[21] The body of work of Muslim savants, translated into Latin, was welcomed in Western universities and helped the backward Europeans of that time to extricate themselves from their decadence and move toward the Renaissance and the scientific and technological revolution.[22]

All of a sudden, the great Islamic civilization came to naught, and after the twelfth century the declining Muslim world never regained its past splendor. There were, to be sure, some fits of accomplishments and by the sixteenth century three Islamic empires were shining: the Mogul (India), the Safavid (Iran), and the Ottoman (Turkey and the Balkans).[23] But the latter, in spite of its military successes in central Europe, failed to produce intellectual achievements and the two others' artistic and philosophical accomplishments were short-lived. By the end of the eighteenth century and during the nineteenth, decadence became steady in the Muslim world and the encounter with a West in full scientific and technological swing proved disastrous. Modernist movements appeared everywhere, claiming the necessity of reforms and the introduction of Western knowledge and institutions. Colonialism exacerbated these movements and triggered new waves of nationalism. At the same time, traditionalist fundamentalists launched their own brand of anti-Western struggle and, more often than not, succeeded in slowing down the pace of change.

In the case of Iran, the attempts to pull the nation out of backwardness started as soon as the mid-nineteenth century with Amir Kabir, brother-in-law of Nassereddin Shah. But at the instigation of feudal landowners and some members of the clergy who dreaded losing their privileges, the Shah ordered his assassination. In the early years of the twentieth century, the constitutionalists won a short-lived victory. In the 1920s and 1930s, Reza Shah followed in the steps of Ataturk, but his reforms came to an end with World War II. Muhammad Reza Shah's White Revolution was dismantled by Khomeini and replaced by a medieval theocracy. The Islamic revolution of 1979, therefore, is in line with the movements that have appeared since the end of the nineteenth century to slow down the pace of modernization or to stop it altogether. Like their predecessors, Khomeini and his followers used the whole arsenal of fundamentalism as well as that of ancient Iranian mythology. The large street demonstrations they organized and their success in overthrowing the traditional institution of monarchy were due to three main factors that did not exist or never compounded in the past: a weak and terminally ill Shah, an early alliance with liberals and intellectuals, and, most importantly, the use of modern communications technology. I shall return to this aspect of the 1979 Islamic revolution later.[24]

Be this as it may, the tension between the twelfth and twentieth centuries, provoked by the ascent of Ayatollah Khomeini, uncovers another enduring feature of Iran's society briefly mentioned in the foregoing: a *basic duality* which one finds in almost all walks of life and society. Thus, dualism is at the heart of Zoroastrianism: Ahura Mazda, the Wise Lord, continually fights Ahriman, the Prince of Darkness. Manicheism, which appeared toward the end of the sixth century, pushed dualism even further and influenced some Muslim thinkers. Iranian dualism is not only a metaphysical feature, it is at work in the nation's three-thousand-year history which can be described as a constant struggle between centralism promoted by the kings and feudality supported by landlords. Having filled the Shah's shoes, Khomeini had to defend centralization. Therefore, one should not be astonished by the bloody ways he used to counter the Kurdish, Baluch, and other provincial autonomist movements.[25]

Since the foundation of the Persian empire by Cyrus, who overthrew the Mede king through a palace revolution, we witness the *endless fight between centralization and feudality*. Darius allied himself with the clergy and subdued the powerful landowners.

Feudality slowly regained the upper hand and weakened the empire, which became easy prey to Alexander's Greek invaders. After the latter's demise, one of his generals, Seleucus, ruled Persia and transferred his capital to Babylon. His maritime provinces rapidly seceded and his rule did not last long. Then the Parths, supported by Zoroastrian clergy, succeeded in patching up the empire into unity but could not resurrect the Achaemenian strong central government. One of their vassals, again with the help of the clergy, founded the powerful Sassanid dynasty and applied a more coherent version of the tripartite ideology (as shown in the aforementioned Tanzar letter to the vassal king of Tabaristan). But the continuous wars with Byzantium once again undermined the central authority of the *Shahinshah*. Iran sunk anew into a long period of anarchy and therefore could not resist the onslaught of Arab Islamized Bedouins.

The Islamic empire, in turn, lost its unity, and the feudals who had reconstituted their large estates in Iran created local dynasties: Tahirids in Khorassan, Saffarids in Sistan, Samanids in Transoxian, Bouids in the South, and so on. After this, two Turkish dynasties, one after another, reestablished a unified Iran: the Ghaznevids and the Seljukids. Notwithstanding their centralizing efforts, both dynasties succumbed to internal rivalries, thus facilitating the conquest by the Mongols. Tamerlane's victory once more frittered away the country. Early in the sixteenth century, Shah Ismail reconstituted the lost unity and founded the Safavid dynasty with Shiite Islam as the state religion and Isfahan as the capital. But during the seventeenth century, the feudal landowners, taking advantage of the wars with the Ottomans and Afghans, unfastened their bonds with Isfahan's court. The unity of Iran was restored again in the beginning of the nineteenth century by the chief of the Qajar tribe who chose Tehran as the capital. By the end of the nineteenth century, the pressure of foreign powers, namely Russia and England, helped the feudals to regain their power. The discovery of oil fields complicated Iranian politics, and the country, after a long period of anarchy, was again unified under the rule of Reza Shah.

REPETITION COMPULSION

In short, the history of Iran evinces an unremitting struggle between the two opposed principles of feudality and centralism, with the Mazdean and later on the Shiite clergy acting as arbiter. Great empires would appear under the authority of powerful kings and crumble later with their weak heirs or in face of foreign invasions. The landowners and tribal chieftains would recapture their total independence until the apparition of a new strong unifier. Moreover, the great kings were always tyrants who leaned on the clergy and practiced cruel repression. The Islamic Republic has certainly not deviated from this ancestral model. Iran's history, therefore, offers the picture of a monotonous concatenation of horrors, as if a mysterious curse had been cast on the whole nation in order to force it to repeat without end the same scenario over and over again. It is as if the whole nation were prey to *repetition compulsion*. The use here of psychiatric terminology seems inescapable. Indeed, how could an entire population submit periodically to totalitarian regimes if it were not suffering from some kind of a *collective neurosis* (if I may use such a phrase)? It is bewildering to see that every time the country reaches a degree of development and well-being, internal and external forces join to bring it back into backwardness and desolation.

It is true that Iranian society, despite these re-starts and setbacks, keeps changing. Not only is today's Iran not comparable to that of ancient times, but it even differs from that of the Qajars and the Pahlavis. Nevertheless, one cannot deny that Iranians seem unable to overcome the ancestral obstacles and hurdles that paralyze them on the road toward progress and always bring them back to case number one. The plight of Iranians reminds one of the Greek legend of Sisyphus who had been compelled to roll a stone to the top of a slope, the stone always escaping him near the top and rolling down again! It also reminds one of what Freud called *fate neurosis*. By this, Freud referred to individuals who were subjected to generally painful experiences which would repeat themselves periodically and appeared to them as imposed from the outside. These experiences unfold according to an immutable scenario.

A number of historians have been stricken by apparent contradictions in the conduct of Iranians. Thus the French historian, René Grousset used to say that the Iranian soul nurtured in its depths specific intellectual undercurrents whose *successive* and *repetitive* manifestations surprise the observer. He cited the following: mazdeism, mazdakism, sufism, extremist Shiite sects, babism, and kashanism.[26] The Iranian soul, he added, contains a mysterious *intellectual anxiety* that compels it to repeat these manifestations. Actually, to attribute this characteristic of Iranian history to a secret tendency of the Iranian soul does not constitute an explanation, it amounts to begging the question! Moreover, if this compulsive repetition were a characteristic of the soul, Iranians would be condemned to repeat forever the same scenario.

Let's see if psychiatry and psychoanalysis can help us in this respect. As I have already indicated, in Freud's *fate neurosis*, specific experiences, generally painful ones, repeat themselves, sometimes over a long period of time. There certainly is a resemblance between these individual repetitive scenarios and the outlook of the historical cycles of Iranian history. The reaction of Iranians to such events also reminds one of the reaction of patients suffering from *fate neurosis*. After each painful episode, people consider that it has been imposed on them by external causes, submit to the quirk of fate, and pray for God to send them a savior. The leaders, for their part, attribute their failures to foreigners' schemes: the mullahs accuse the Great Satan (United States); the Shah, the oil companies.

To psychiatrists the causes of *fate neurosis* are buried in the unconscious of the patient. This seems to confirm what I said about the powerful influence of old myths in the *psyche* of Iranians. Indeed, legendary stories are implanted in the minds of children by their mothers, nannies, storytellers, elementary school teachers, and so on.[27] It is as if ancient mythology were the fabric of Iranians' *collective unconscious*.

Mainstream psychoanalysts consider that beyond its demonic aspect, *fate neurosis* is a manifestation of *repetition compulsion* and *defense mechanisms* that result in the perpetuation of some rigid character trait of the patient. If one tries to extend this explanation of a particular neurosis to the level of an entire society (in this case the Iranian society), one can say that the particular unconscious *defense mechanisms* help to maintain a traditional form of governance and social conduct. The repetitive cycles of Iranian history show, if anything, that their mythological motivations have played (and continue to play) a role similar to that of *defense mechanisms* in psychoanalysis. This tendency of Iranians to repeat in certain circumstances the patterns of some of their mythological stories has served as a safeguard for their national cultural identity. Each time that a foreign element (invasion or interference) or an internal cause (reforms or, since the nineteenth century, modernization) would threaten the traditional order, the mythological *defense mechanism* would be almost automatically unleashed, as in the case of an individual's *fate neurosis*.

Iranians are generally proud of their successful resistance in the face of all the vicissitudes of history. Yet they forget to evaluate the cost of such a curious system of defense which results in, so to say, congealing their society in the remote past. The result of this method of defense has been in the past to eternalize feudality and in present times to stop the necessary changes in the ways of life and social institutions. I dare say that it is because of their ignorance of these unconscious mechanisms that the Iranian modernizers have been losers up to now. To succeed in bringing Iran into modern times, one has to change the *mind-set* of Iranians and at the same time the material infrastructure of their society. The modernizers took care of the latter and did nothing to change the *mind-set*. As for Khomeini and his Islamic Republic, the catastrophic balance sheet of the regime clearly underlines the exorbitant and outrageous price of the efforts to keep the Islamic fundamentalist identity of Iranian society in the twenty-first century! This is not the place here to consider the merits and shortcomings of the Western model of development or the failures of modernity: that is a matter for specialists and experts to take up when they will draw the programs of a post-Khomeini Iran. What is clear in the perspective of this book, is that fundamentalism constitutes as costly and catastrophic a *defense mechanism* as the *repetition compulsion* of neurotic patients.

The foregoing shows that one cannot understand the Islamic revolution of 1979 without considering the enduring mythology of ancient Persia. Conversely, the Islamic coloration of the 1979 revolution has also had an influence in the unfolding of events. Although Iranian Shiism is steeped in Iran's pre-Islamic past, it nevertheless is also a part of Islam's history. To understand more accurately Khomeini's revolution in Iran, one must consider it both in the context of Iranian as well Islamic mythologies and history.

CHAPTER THREE

The Unwritten Constitution and the "Hidden Imam"

In the last two months of 1978, the huge crowds marching in Tehran's main arteries and regularly shouting "Allah Akbar" (Allah is the greatest), flabbergasted foreign observers. The crowd's vibrant religious fervor tended to conceal all other aspects of the events. To the amazed journalists, the faithful repeated invariably: "We all are Muslims. There is no difference between us!"[1] Even the nonbelievers and intellectual atheists affirmed that all religious demands were not retrograde and, Muslims or not, they all were fighting for freedom and against dictatorship.[2] Moreover, the swarming throngs assembled by Khomeini's followers around Tehran's Mehrabad airport on February 1, 1979, to witness the return from exile of the old ayatollah, reinforced the impression that religion was the prime mover of the revolution. Commentators all over the world wrote and spoke about a so-called awakening of Islam, as if Muslims had been engulfed in slumber for centuries. In fact, Muslims had always continued to practice their religion with the meticulousness of a clock. The deviations one would find in large cities were far from being novel. Indeed, in the first decades of Islam, there were already Muslims who drank wine (The Caliph Umar punished his own son for drunkenness!); women who did not cover their hair; men who did not fast during the month of Ramadan; merchants who cheated their patrons; and chronicles containing reports about numerous thieves whose hands were severed and adulterous spouses who were stoned to death. Today, as in the past, turpitudes exist everywhere in Muslim countries. Even in Saudi Arabia, rich people drink and watch satellite-transmitted Western movies behind the walls of their swanky villas. The same happens in the Islamic Republic of Iran, where the occasional raids by the *Pasdarans* (Revolutionary Guards) and other *Hezbollah* thugs have only succeeded in creating a thriving bootlegging industry and giving Tehran the appearance of the 1930s Chicago, save for political freedoms.

I have briefly indicated in the previous chapter that the fundamentalist interpretations of the Koran triumphed in the twelfth century and remained valid thereafter. What Khomeini succeeded in awakening was not Islam, but rather *militant Islam* which actually is nothing else but *fundamentalism in action*. The militants pretend to impose Islamic law and mores in the strictest ways in public as well as private life. Since the nineteenth century, because of expanding contacts with the West, such inflexibility was rather on the wane in Muslim countries and militant Islam was confined to small groups such as the Egyptian Muslim Brotherhood or the Iranian *Fedayin-e-Islam*, who practiced oral or written propaganda and sometimes assassinations or other acts of violence. Khomeini made fundamentalism a doctrine of government and, as a result, encouraged similar movements in all the Muslim world, including countries like Turkey that had imposed secularism for many decades.

In the previous chapter I have also alluded to the pre-Islamic origins of Khomeini's absolutist and totalitarian regime. I intend now to examine the Islamic revolution in the framework of the mythology and history of Islam in general and Iranian Shiism in particular.

ISLAM'S FIRST CENTURY

Less than a century after its birth, Islam became the dominant religion in vast territories extending from the Indian Ocean to the Atlantic. It took a traveler riding a camel (the most rapid means of transportation in those days) some 18 months to trek across the Muslim empire. The caravans that crisscrossed it in all directions transported silk, carpets, incense, spices, and a host of other staples. In the folds of brocade and cashmere fabrics one would find mathematical treatises from India, astronomical tables from Persia, translations of the works of Aristotle and Plato from Syria. Medical students learned Arabic in order to read the works of Hippocrates at the University of Montpellier. Western scholars flocked to Córdoba, where the library contained over one hundred thousand manuscripts.

Islam, which constituted the only link between the ethnically different inhabitants of this vast empire, started in Arabia's desert where the archangel Gabriel revealed God's last message to Muhammad. This was the first night of the month of Ramadan. (According to legend, every year on the first of that month, heaven's doors open and God hears the prayers of humans.) Back in Mecca, Muhammad recounted his fantastic experience, but, save for a handful of relatives and friends, people did not believe and rather scorned him before starting to persecute his followers. The Prophet and the faithful fled to Medina, converted all Arabia's tribes in less than two decades, and returned triumphantly to Mecca.

The gist of the new religion was quite simple. One would become a Muslim by reciting the phrase: There is no God but Allah and Muhammad is His envoy. The believer should also pray five times a day, fast the whole month of Ramadan, pay a voluntary contribution, and accomplish the pilgrimage to Mecca (if he could afford the expenses). In addition, God expected that Muslims would fight in order to spread his message all over the world. This is the jihad (holy war) which Muhammad himself conducted in Arabia and, after his demise, the caliphs continued. Jihad's participants are neither mercenaries nor ordinary soldiers. They are committed believers who are ready to sacrifice their own lives for the success of the cause. They were told that God likes martyrs and opens to them the gates of paradise without waiting for the final judgment. (This is almost exactly the language Ayatollah Khomeini used to overthrow the Shah, repel the Iraqi army, and try to spread Islamic revolution outside Iran.)

Prophet Muhammad died in A.D. 632 without having put rules in place about his succession as head of the state created in Medina. Consequently, immediately after his demise, a fierce struggle for power pitted his companions one against the other. The majority of the people of Medina opted for the Bedouin tradition of election and designated Abu Bakr, Muhammad's father-in-law. But, a minority were in favor of his cousin and son-in-law Ali. Thus, division appeared among Muslims in the very early stages of the development of the religion. Abu Bakr died of old age, and his successors Umar and Uthman were assassinated. When Ali finally became caliph, Muawya, a relative of Uthman and governor of Syria, waged war against him. Ali was also murdered and Muawya proclaimed himself caliph and created the hereditary dynasty of the Ummayads with Damascus as his capital. In the meantime, Ali's son Hussein revolted and was killed in the desert of Kerbela. This event reinforced the supporters of Ali who accused the Ummayads of having dared to suppress the Prophet's grandson. It also hardened the incipient divisions among Muslims. Very soon the faithful were definitely split between Sunnites (majority) and Shiites (minority). The Shiites fleeing repression found refuge in Persia, especially in the province of Khorassan, where anti-Arab feelings were strong. Indeed, the Iranians, who possessed a refined civilization and elaborate spiritual antecedents (Zoroastrianism), ran rings around the Bedouin invaders. They lent support to Ali's followers and helped to create the cult of Hussein, whom they dubbed Prince of Martyrs. The Shiites opposed the Ummayads based on the legitimacy of the Prophet's family.

The revolt against the Ummayads started in Khorassan and gave birth to the Abbassid dynasty, which shifted the capital of the Muslim empire from Damascus to Baghdad. Notwithstanding the essential contribution of the Shiites to their victory, the Abbassids soon turned against them. The sect went underground and transformed itself from a political movement into a full-fledged theological one that spread rapidly in the Muslim world.

SHIISM AND ITS DIFFERENCES FROM SUNNISM

The Sunnites follow the literal meaning of the Koran, which, among other teachings, affirms clearly that Muhammad is the seal of prophecy, meaning that he is the last envoy. After him God will send no other Prophet. Therefore, the Koran is the last message of God. That is why all Muslims, including Shiites, consider the *Sharia* (Islamic law) as final and unalterable; there can be no revision or evolution of the Sharia.

Shiites do not contest this interpretation. They accept Muhammad as the seal and the *Sharia* as eternal, but they affirm that the Koran, in addition to its literal meaning has a hidden one that escapes ordinary men. Only a spiritual guide—an Imam—can gradually reveal the secrets of the Koran, at diverse periods in time when he considers that men are ready to understand it. Citing a *hadith* (a saying attributed to the Prophet), the Shiites profess that Muhammad had designated Ali and his male descendants for the role of Imam, and that is why the caliphate should have been bestowed on Ali and his descendants. Therefore, the first three caliphs as well as the Ummayads were usurpers and lacked legitimacy. The Sunnites, for their part, contest the existence of the *hadith* quoted by the Shiites and therefore reject the whole Shiite doctrine.[3]

The 12th Imam mysteriously disappeared during his infancy, interrupting the line of descendants of the Imams. In the theological view of the duodecimal Shiites, the 12th Imam is not dead; he continues to live among humans but remains invisible to them. He is the *Mahdi* (messiah) promised by Prophet Muhammad who is to reestablish the reign of justice and true faith on earth. He will certainly reappear one day and Shiites are waiting for him with utmost fervor. In his absence, the Doctors of Law (also called *faghihs*, theologians, *ulama*) must maintain and protect the faith. The most savants among them become ayatollahs, and the most sage among the ayatollahs receive the title of *majra-e-taqulid* (source of imitation), meaning that the believers must follow their indications and rulings in order to remain on the right path. Obviously, the ayatollahs cannot reveal new meanings of the Koran and, in the absence of the 12th Imam, can only repeat the meanings revealed by the eleven Imams. The 12th Imam, who went into hiding in A.D. 878, will reappear to the sight of Muslims when their hearts and consciences will become capable of recognizing him. At such a time he will govern earth with justice and assure the happiness of real Muslims. That is why he is dubbed Master of Time and *Mahdi* (messiah).

It is important to point out that the Shiite doctrine (also called Imamism) reminds one of some of the ideas developed by Zoroaster and contained in Mazdeism (which was the religion of all Iranians before the Arab conquest). Indeed, Zoroastrianism, which is older than the Abrahamic religions, announced the coming of a savior, Shoshyant, who would arrange for the triumph of the forces of good over those of evil. As already indicated in the previous chapter, this state of lying in wait for the coming of a savior is one of the constants of the mind-set of Iranians since time immemorial. This attitude often confuses foreign observers who believe that Iranians are skeptical by nature and therefore not prone to fanaticism. In fact they can be as fanatic as any other human group. The *Hezbollah*'s recruits have proven it since the Islamic revolution, and the ayatollah himself with his death sentence against the British writer Rushdie.

The title of Imam bestowed by the throngs and the press on Khomeini since his arrival from exile on February 1, 1979, has created some ambiguity. In Shiism, Imam means guide in the title of the Saint Imams: Ali and his eleven descendants. Nobody can equate with them, and the religious authority of Khomeini cannot go beyond that of other grand ayatollahs. But in Arabic, Imam means the one who stands before, especially at the Friday prayer in a mosque. Imam can also signify a sage capable of offering guidance in current affairs of the believers. In the case of Khomeini, it meant that he was considered as the guide of the revolution. But, in their minds, many uneducated Iranians thought that he actually was the reincarnation of the Hidden Imam. Khomeini himself used to say that he represented the awaited Imam or *Mahdi*. All this produced a state of confusion about the ayatollah's status and role.[4]

The cult of the Imams in Iranian Shiism sometimes goes even beyond that of the Prophet! Sunnites accuse Shiites of heresy in this respect. Indeed, to them Muhammad is the seal of Prophets and the Koran the last religious law; Allah has put nobody between Himself and the faithful (there is no priesthood in mainstream Islam). To such arguments, Shiites respond that in reappearing, the 12th Imam will not bring a new religious law but will only reveal the esoteric meaning of the Koran; The Imams are not prophets, but only the trustees of the hidden meanings of God's message.

Shiism is not confined to Iran as is currently thought by a great number of persons. It first appeared in mostly Arab environment and exists today in almost all Muslim countries, including Saudi Arabia (the stronghold of orthodox Sunnism), as a minority group. It was chosen as the state religion in Iran by the Safavid dynasty in the sixteenth century. Some experts affirm that the exaggerated cult of the Imams in Iran is in fact a kind of disguised defense in face of religious thinking brought in by non-Iranians. These observers point out elements of Shiism which remind them of ancient Iranian traditions.

Be this as it may, Iranians have woven many legendary stories around the persons of the Imams in order to link them to their own culture. For instance, according to some of these stories, Imam Hussein, the martyred grandson of the Prophet, married one of the daughters of Yazdeguerd, the last Sassanid king: therefore some Iranian blood flows in the arteries of the nine other Imams! Moreover, Arabs persecuted the Imams and the Shiites; national feelings pervade religious beliefs in Iran. Even Khomeini, who favored Islamic identity over local identity, called on Iranian patriotism in the war against Iraq in the early 1980s. Moreover, many non-Muslim or non-Shiite Iranians venerate the Imams and mourn on the anniversary of Hussein's death.

THE UNWRITTEN CONSTITUTIONAL LAW

The belief in the occultation and eventual return of the 12th Imam is of paramount importance in order to understand the rapidity and almost peaceful fall of the Shah and Khomeini's access to political power. The Hidden Imam is supposed to reappear and establish a just and equitable government on earth. The Prophet was the head of the Muslim state installed in Medina, and the Imams were charged with the duty of continuing his leadership. Therefore, during the absence of the 12th Imam, any government lacks legitimacy because all powers belong to him. When a representative of the Hidden Imam (Ayatollah Khomeini) knocks at the door of the house (Iran) he should be immediately admitted because the provisional occupant of the house (the shah) is in any case a usurper. In Iran this religiously inspired theory is tantamount to an unwritten constitutional law.

After the fall of the Persian empire at the hands of Muslim armies, Ali and his direct descendants succeeded both the Prophet and the Iranian monarch. As a consequence, the three first caliphs and those who rose after the short-lived caliphate of Ali, as well as all the Muslim leaders of the past and the present, *were or are illegitimate.* They were or are governing de facto, not de jure. Khomeini made no effort to proclaim his own legitimacy. Indeed, he affirmed without modesty that after the death of the Prophet and before his accession to power in Iran, real Islam was applied nowhere on earth.

A question arises at this juncture: Why, notwithstanding this unwritten constitutional law, do Shiites obey and carry out the orders of secular leaders whom they consider as mere usurpers? The explanation can be found in the old theory of fathership. A father is necessary in a household, a father capable of dealing with the daily current affairs and of ensuring external and internal security. It can happen that the usurper serves the people well and attracts their sympathy and gratitude, despite his basic illegitimacy. Moreover, the identity and origins of the usurper (the de facto head of state) is of no importance. In the absence of the Hidden Imam anybody can occupy the seat of government. Reza Shah, for instance, was not of aristocratic origin, nor were some of the adventurers who ascended the Peacock throne for a short time. The people had to tolerate these fathers who brought some order and justice, but they did not bestow legitimacy on their rule. The palaces and all their contents were not their property but that of the absent Imam. Iranian clerics have always strictly limited their contacts with the shahs. They were reluctant to enter the palaces unduly occupied by them. It is reported that when a high-ranking cleric was forced to visit one of the Qajar shahs, he lifted the carpet, refused the offered chair, and sat on the floor. Since all these objects were stolen by the Shah, religion forbids their use to the faithful.[5] For the same reason, Iranian clerics did not accept any gift from the monarchs. But they never refused the money provided by the prime minister, because it came out of the public treasury and not from the Shah's coffer.

The Iranian monarchs, for their part, always tried their best to link themselves in one manner or another to the Saint Imams. Thus, Nassereddin Shah Qajar, whose reign lasted for almost half a century, pretended that he possessed an authentic portrait of Ali, the first Imam. Mohammad Reza Pahlavi affirmed that the eighth Imam (Reza) had saved him from death in his childhood. In his book, *Toward the Great Civilization,* he declared: "The numerous extraordinary events of my life have convinced me that a Heavenly Force directs my fate (destiny) on the path she has determined. Everything I accomplish is inspired by this Force. . . ."[6]

Notwithstanding all these pretensions and claims about contacts with heaven and the Imams, the illegitimacy of monarchy as stated in the unwritten constitutional law remained in force. Even the Safavid kings, who had made Shiism the official religion of the state, could not curry favor with the clergy, who considered them as usurpers like any other Shah. Against this backdrop, Khomeini acted and brought in his own interpretation of the unwritten constitution, which differed from that of other ayatollahs. Going further than his fundamentalist teachers, he proclaimed during his exile that the *faghihs* have the *right and even the duty* to seize power and direct the government, despite the fact that it belongs to the Hidden Imam.[7] His line of reasoning was quite simple: the wielding of power by the ayatollahs and the clergy would safeguard the integrity of the religious law with which the Shah was tampering.

This, in turn, he added, would pave the way for the return of the 12th Imam. He developed this thesis in his lessons in Najaf.[8]

One is confounded by the simplistic reasoning of the ayatollah. He says that since Allah has not designated anybody to govern in the absence of the 12th Imam, He therefore implied that the virtues of Islamic governments up to the 12th Imam must be perpetuated. These virtues are a perfect knowledge of law and justice, which exist in many members of the the clergy. If the latter would unite they could lay the basis of a government capable of ensuring universal justice. If a competent person appears with the intention of forming an Islamic government, he must have been invested by God with the same mandate as the Prophet to guide the people. In that case, it is the duty of the people to obey him.

In another context, Khomeini riled those who speak of secular government. Only atheists want to separate state and religion. Politics and religion were not kept apart in the lifetime of the Prophet! Such ideas are aberrations invented by imperialists in order to keep the clergy away from the material and social life of Muslim peoples and to steal their riches more easily. To ensure the unity of Muslims and liberate the Islamic world from the domination of imperialists, high-ranking clerics must form an Islamic government in Iran, overthrow the tyrannical rulers supported by foreigners, and then, install the universal authority of Islam.

The political views of Ayatollah Khomeini, as exposed in his books, are rather simplistic. He aims, as it were, to fill administratively the governmental void which has existed since the disappearance of the 12th Imam. The ayatollahs in general, and himself in particular, possess the virtues and qualities that the Prophet, as head of the Medina state, demanded of his companions and collaborators. Therefore, they can take charge of the highest positions of governance. The separation of powers in modern constitutional laws is but a diabolical imperialist invention concocted only for the purpose of plundering the riches of Muslim countries and eventually erasing Islam from the surface of the planet. In order to overcome this devilish plan and reconstitute the unity of the Muslim world, the clergy must act resolutely and gather in its hands all the strings of government.

Khomeini failed in 1963 because in those days his discourse was too complicated for the masses to understand. Moreover, he, a son, was confronting the Shah who was considered the father of the nation. In 1978, his words were crystal clear and therefore accessible to the throngs. Islam seemed in real danger as the Shah had rejected the Islamic calendar, replacing it with one starting at the foundation of the first Iranian empire by Cyrus the Great. The Shah was also abandoning the harsh features of the traditional father. Finally, Khomeini was presenting himself as the representative of the Hidden Imam and accepting the title of Imam his followers had bestowed on him.

POPULISM AND FUNDAMENTALISM

Not unlike the Shah before him (at least in his books), the old ayatollah pretended to accomplish a divinely inspired mission. He therefore had the right and the duty to overthrow the Iranian monarchy and provoke revolts against the pseudo-Muslim leaders of other lands in order to hasten the reapparition of the 12th Imam and the establishment of God's reign on the entire planet. The success of his enterprise is quite natural among people who, like Iranians, lay in wait for the Zoroastrian Shoshyant before the advent of Islam and for the Shiite Hidden Imam thereafter.

Most Western commentators attributed the fall of the Shah to the "widespread misery" of the Iranian people. In fact, in 1978, for the first time after many centuries, Iranians did not suffer from hunger: over-employment had prompted the import of foreign workers and created inflation! It is indeed one of the most curious characteristics of the Islamic revolution that it was not a revolt of downtrodden and starving throngs. Even more curious was the fact that despite its religious flavor, it did not aim at introducing a spiritual dimension into politics as some Western observers thought.[9] Notwithstanding its religious flavor, it was in fact a class warfare in the sense that the cleric class aimed at replacing the political class.

It is true that one cannot measure poverty by only the standard of daily diet. Corruption and contemptuous luxury of the upper classes underlined the gap between their income and that of a great part of the people. Moreover, the presence of foreigners in general, and Americans in particular, irritated many Iranians. Rapid economic development, rural exodus toward cities, and the invasion of Western fashions (due to the increase of income and the spread of modern means of communications) changed the social scenery. It was as if imitation of Western ways was dangerously threatening traditional ways of life.

Khomeini's speeches, taped on cassettes and distributed by his followers, entranced people, especially in the lower classes. Indeed, the ayatollah, contrary to intellectuals and polititicians, used the common language and talked of the daily problems of the masses: inflation and rising prices, military expenses, luxury spending of the rich, squandering of the oil revenues, corruption of the royal family and the courtiers, and so on. Shrewdly enough, the ayatollah studded his down-to-earth sayings with small doses of his political ideas about an Islamic government. He accused the Shah of collusion with Israel. He added that real Islam had never been practiced after the Prophet and after the first Imam (Ali); his Islamic government, the first after that of Ali, would distribute the revenues of oil to the people while the Shah and his foreign protectors used to steal them; the clerics would ensure social justice; Allah would open the gates of paradise to those who would fight for the establishment of a real Islamic government; the Hidden Imam, satisfied with the observance of Islamic law, would hasten his return. In a sly, calculating way, the old ayatollah combined and wove together material and religious objectives.

The populist elements thus used by Khomeini and his followers put the fat in the fire. The masses thought they had not only nothing to lose, but a lot to gain. Khomeini's words whetted their never fully satisfied material appetite. At the same time, the religious content animated their belief in the sanctity of the Imams. On top of that, the anti-Semitic allusions in the revolutionary propaganda suited the Iranians, who, only a few years back, had manifested their hate for Israel in the framework of the Asian soccer games: after the victory of the Iranian team over Israel, the enthusiastic mob took to the streets chanting anti-Jewish slogans. Already in his lessons and books, the ayatollah did not spare the Jews. Thus, in *Kashf-ol-Asrar* one can find a passage in which he accused them of colluding with the Christians, the imperialists, and the atheists, in order to constitute a universal Jewish state and expunge Islam from the world.[10] "He also accused the Shah of allowing Christian and Bahai centers of propaganda in Tehran in which the truths of the Koran were falsified. Khomeini's militant fundamentalism rested therefore on two pillars: on the one hand, it agitated the specter of a danger menacing Islam, and on the other hand it used the entire arsenal of populism. On its first pillar, it pretended to profess God's truth.

What is this truth? Islam being the final message of Allah, supersedes all other religions, and all humanity should convert to it. Therefore, the spread of Islam is a basic commandment of God. To accomplish it, Muslims should resume the jihad (holy war) and this time pursue it until total victory. Moreover, Islam covers all aspects of life and society. Out of the 50 volumes that collect the *hadiths* (sayings of the Prophet), only four discuss prayer and the duties of the faithful toward his creator. All the rest is devoted to economic, legal, social, and political problems.[11] The strict application of the *Sharia* will provide Muslims with justice and happiness. As *ulama* and *faghihs* are the sole experts in matter of religion, everybody should obey them. Their interpretations of the divine message (meaning the Koran) constitute the compelling truth for all. Curiously enough, on this level, Shiism and Sunnism have no basic differences. That is why, though a Shiite, Ayatollah Khomeini enjoys great respect among Sunnite masses. On the populist level, disillusion came rapidly as it always happens in the case of seizure of power by any extremist group. The populists, once in power, can never deliver all the promises they made in order to lure in the people.

One more reason for the astounding success of the Islamic revolution lies in the fact that many people were afraid of "missing the boat": they jumped into it, hoping to share its projected profits. In this respect I would like to cite a popular story from Persian folklore, which might help us to better understand this aspect of Khomeini's victory over the Shah.

MULLAH NASSEREDDIN'S RUSE

A little while before his dismissal as prime minister, Mehdi Bazargan, head of the provisional government, said seriously to a foreign journalist: "In truth the Ayatollah has always despised mullahs, but since his return he is under their influence."[12] I don't know where this ex-liberal and pro-Mossadegh politician had picked up such an opinion about his new master. Yet, if the ayatollah was not opposed to the mullahs, there was at least one he despised and rejected. Although that cleric had left this world long ago, his repute had braved centuries and acquired mythical dimensions. People of all classes still enjoy his witticisms. His name was Mullah Nassereddin. His piety and deep knowledge of religion had won him the title of mullah. Unwilling to deceive his countrymen, he used to go to the mosque on Fridays and don the prescribed mantle and turban. One of his adventures might help us better understand the causes of Ayatollah Khomeini's success.

At the time of the incident, the country had been at war for some time with one of its neighbors. As a result, it was suffering many shortages, especially in food. One day Mullah Nassereddin went to the market to buy bread, and a long line was waiting at the door of the bakery. Knowing quite well the character and mind-set of his fellow citizens, Nassereddin thought of a dodge. He addressed the throng with these words: "O honorable friends, why are you losing your time waiting at the door of this bakery while at the nearby grocery they are distributing rice gratuitously?" The line broke instantly and restarted at the door of the other store. As he was about to enter the bakery, Nassereddin, looking at the people patiently waiting at the grocery's door, had second thoughts. After all, it could be that at the behest of the Imam, who wanted to quench popular discontent, the grocery was offering free rice. Nassereddin left the bakery and joined the line at the grocery.

To come back to the Islamic revolution, Ayatollah Khomeini's populist discourse had touched, as it were, people's avidity chord. They had in mind the fabulous oil revenues which were stolen by the Shah and the rich. If the thieves were expelled, all these riches would fall in the basket of the people. The masses believed Khomeini's words and joined his revolution. But as I have emphasized before, the bait of material gain alone cannot explain the outcome of the upheaval. While exploiting and blowing the horn at every source of discontent, Khomeini never forgot his basic objectives and continued to insist on the dangers threatening true Islam. Even now, more than 20 years after its birth, the leaders of the Islamic regime see everywhere around them menacing dangers lurking in the dark. They go as far as setting up straw opponents. They point their fingers at supposed enemies of the religion that should be suppressed: imperialists, modernists, Jews, leaders of Arab countries, Christians, Bahais, atheists, intellectuals, journalists, students, and so on. Agents of the Great Satan (United States) and smaller Satans are glaring at the purity of the Islamic Republic. You are for or against Allah: there is no middle. Under these conditions, the sole party a Muslim can join is the *Hezbollah* (Party of God). All the others are opposed to the creator, and are therefore allies of the devil. That is why Khomeini finally ordered the dissolution of the Party of the Islamic Republic he had himself helped to create in 1979. Despite its name the *Hezbollah* is not a structured political organization. It includes groups of people who act inside and outside Iran against the so-called enemies of God, taking hostages, resorting to terrorism, using intimidation, and so on. Their objective is the defense of Islam while waiting for the jihad to resume.

In the case of Iran, as early as 1976–77, Khomeini's followers launched rumors about the Shah's intention, with the help of Israel, to restore Zoroastrianism as the official religion of Iran. During the revolution, they used the Soviet methods of misinformation. They spread, for instance, rumors about supposed Israeli soldiers donning Iranian uniforms and shooting at peaceful demonstrators.

International media, under the pretext of informing the world, amplified the Khomeini propaganda: showing again and again the same crowd chanting Allah Akbar; interviewing Khomeini and his entourage; and boasting that this was the first revolution entirely unfolding in front of the TV cameras. All this helped create the impression that the Iranian revolution was something absolutely original in the history of Islam and of the world! In reality, the slogan "Islam in danger" had been used by many others before Khomeini: The Almoravids and Almohads in North Africa and Andalusia in the twelfth century, Saladin in Egypt in the twelfth century and the *Mahdi* in Sudan in the nineteenth century.

The TV images of the Islamic revolution nurtured another delusion in the minds of the viewers: many attributed some kind of extraordinary mobilizing quality to Islam, failing to notice that it was the slogan "Islam in danger" that excited the masses. Khomeini himself understood this nuance only after his first uprising against the Shah in the 1960s. He did not speak then of "Islam in danger," and he lost his bid against the monarch. A glance at the history of Islam will further clarify this point.

ISLAM AND FUNDAMENTALISM

When the Muslim horsemen took off from the Arabian desert and invaded the Greco-Roman and Persian empires, they came into contact with two great and sophisticated civilizations—a far cry from their simple and unrefined Bedouin mores. Not only did they not reject them as non-Islamic, but they embraced them and adopted their congeries of knowledge and inventions, their political institutions and more often than not their lifestyles. Being just a handful of warriors compared to the large populations of these lands, they ruled their newly founded empire by leaning on the local administrations and civil servants. The relatively liberal (for those times) atmosphere that ensued favored the recovery of intellectual activities, which had been strictly stifled by the absolutism of Byzantine and Sassanid regimes. Thirst for new knowledge and creativity blossomed anew in all fields. Not only the local religions (Christianity, Judaism, Zoroastrianism) were tolerated, but a kind of dialogue between them and Islam flourished. Even inside Islam itself several schools of thought grew up. Science and philosophy thrived with the adoption of Indian mathematics, Greek thought, Persian astronomy, and so on. Very quickly a new great civilization took shape and extended from the Indus River to the Atlantic Ocean. But by the end of the eleventh century, it started to decline as rapidly as it had started, while at the same time the West was slowly beginning its gradual ascent toward Renaissance.

How can one account for such a swift rise and slump? To be sure, there are many political, economic, social, and cultural causes. Muslim as well as Western historians have tackled the problem in a host of scholarly studies. In my opinion, most of them, if not all, do not give enough importance to the political background of the struggle for power that spread inside the Muslim world around the end of the eleventh century and during the whole twelfth century, that ended with the triumph of fundamentalist interpretations of the Koran. If in its early years the Muslim world was characterized by a great openness to other cultures, it suddenly rejected them together with most of its own findings and closed itself to all and any new outside contribution and influence. Philosophically speaking, Islamic theology became stultified in a fundamentalist and legalistic interpretation of the religion that stopped all progress.

What happened then was a political process that developed in vast parts of the empire. At the peak of Muslim civilization, the non-Arab people who converted to Islam constituted the great majority of the population and resented Arab domination. Their upper classes longed for the most important political posts, traditionally reserved to Arab Muslims. The only way open to the contenders (Turks, Persians, Berbers, and others) was to present themselves as *more Muslim* than the Arab rulers and to accuse the latter of laxity in enforcing Allah's commandments and therefore of *endangering Islam* as a religion.[13] Therefore they adhered to the most fundamentalist interpretations and protected the most extremist clerics who anathematized their more moderate colleagues. Thus, for instance, in Iran and Mesopotamia, the Seljukids (second half of the eleventh century) revived al-Asha'ri's theology, and in North Africa and Andalusia the Almohads (second half of the twelfth century) leaned on Ibn Tumart's interpretations. Both these theologians condemned the influences of pre-Islamic Greek and Persian philosophers as well as the so-called natural scientists.

As a result, by the twelfth century the Muslim world had been stripped of the intellectual drive that fires up research and thinking on the path of knowledge and progress. In the eastern part of the Muslim world the Seljukids (of Turkish origin), accepted as protectors of the Abbassid Caliph of Baghdad, waged a war against all heretics, including the philosophers, and resumed the jihad against Christians in Asia Minor. They created an official university in Baghdad to spread fundamentalism. They burned impious books and executed or exiled their authors. A little later the same scenario unfolded in the western part of the Muslim world, with the ascent of the Almohad dynasty in Morocco and Andalusia.

This triumph of religious fundamentalism struck a fatal blow to the entire Islamic civilization, which never recovered, despite the military successes of the Ottomans in the eighteenth and early nineteenth centuries. The strict interpretations that became official in those days are still valid and in place today. Thus, to quote only two examples, nonmedical books by Avicenna and Averroes remain forbidden. As I have indicated in the previous chapter, what took place in the twelfth century was tantamount to a *cultural suicide*. Yet, Muslim science did not disappear. It was gathered by Western scholars who pursued the quests of Muslim sages in their universities. In the Muslim world, thinking, as it were, took refuge in the secrecy of mystic societies. But the activities of the Sufis and other mystics, though producing some remarkable poems and philosophical treatises, did not alter the general trend of decline. The hunt for blasphemous writers and thinkers never stopped. Even today, fanatics kill intellectuals at the behest or with the approbation of high-ranking clerics. It suffices to cite here the famous case of Rushdie condemned to death by Khomeini's *fatwa* (religious ruling)!

Against this permanent fundamentalist backdrop, Ayatollah Khomeini prepared and launched his Islamic revolution in Iran in order to seize the political power. A question then arises as to how and why the liberal intellectuals of Iran (and their leftist colleagues in the West) defended Khomeini and thought that with his help they would replace the Shah's dictatorship with a democratic regime.

THE DOUBLE TALK

The ayatollah's totalitarian concept of government had been clearly described in at least one of his books titled *Islamic Government (Hokoumat-e-Islami)* in which he affirmed that such a government is instituted by God, whose law is eternal and therefore cannot be changed or disputed; contrary to other systems where the representatives of the people or of the state submit and vote laws, in Islam, God is the only authority; the legislative power belongs to the Prophet and after him to a council of clerics who transmit to each department the Islamic laws and instructions concerning it; Koranic eternal laws must be obeyed by everybody; people obey the Prophet because God has ordered it; for the same reason they must obey the leaders of the Islamic government.

It is true that such a totalitarian conception did not evince in Khomeini's declarations when he had taken refuge in Neauphle-le-Chateau, near Paris, in September 1978. There he insisted that his only goal was the overthrow of the Shah and his regime and their replacement by a *real constitutional government.* "The religious dignitaries do not want to rule."[14] A year later he proclaimed, "Those who pretend that religious dignitaries should not rule, poison the atmosphere and combat against Iran's interests."[15]

In Neauphle-le-Chateau, he promised that "the Islamic government will answer criticism by reason and logic."[16] Less than one year later he menaced: "I repeat for the last time: abstain from holding meetings, from blathering, from publishing protests. Otherwise I will break your teeth."[17]

His entourage followed suit. Thus Ibrahim Yazdi, an American Iranian who later became his foreign minister before heading a political group, told Henry Precht, at the time head of the State Department's Iranian desk, that after the Shah all political parties and the press would enjoy total freedom of expression and would even be allowed to criticize Islam.[18] Ghotbzadeh, an early companion and also a foreign minister (who was later executed), wrote in a French daily, "the new Iranian regime, based on Islamic learning and experiences dating back to the time of the Prophet and Imam Ali, will offer total liberty to everybody."[19]

One can quote inumerable contradictory declarations by Ayatollah Khomeini and his entourage. But the few mentioned above suffice for the purpose of this chapter. In fact, there is no domain in which the ayatollah did not use double talk. Was he trying to deceive his followers and the Iranian people? He obviously wanted to accommodate his allies among the liberals, seculars, and intellectuals for the simple reason that, in 1978, he needed them in order to achieve his goal of overthrowing the Shah and seizing power. From his point of view, he was not proffering lies; he was only resorting to the art of double talk. This usual Iranian practice is called *ketman* in religious terms and *taghieh* in current language. The mullahs pretend that this is nothing other than discretion, which was recommended by the Saint Imams to the Shiites in order to escape the persecutions imposed on them by the Sunnites. But as far as Iran is concerned, the practice of double talk existed long before Islam.

LICIT MENDACITY

In the case of Shiism, *ketman* is not only a safeguard, but also a device commanded by respect for the hidden meanings of the scriptures which should not be revealed to persons unable to understand and honor them; indeed, it would be a spiritual betrayal to entrust the sacred truth to the unworthy or infidel. In any case, one should hide his real opinions from the enemy of religion and try his best to deceive him.

As stated earlier, Ayatollah Khomeini believed that he was accomplishing a divine secret mission. To overthrow the Shah, he needed a coalition of all the opponents, including the liberals and the communists. The revelation of his real goal (establishment of a theocracy) would have made any alliance impossible. Therefore, it was imperative that the old ayatollah hide his real intentions and tell everyone exactly what they wanted to hear. An old Persian saying advises the faithful to conceal the truth instead of creating dissension. Among Western experts, the nineteenth-century French diplomat-writer Gobineau is one of the very few who understood the importance and meaning of *ketman* in Iran.[20]

In Neauphle-le-Chateau, near Paris, Khomeini repeated constantly that the envisioned Islamic government would ensure freedom of thought and expression to all Iranians, including infidels, communists, and ethnic and religious minorities. He also hailed the role of women in the revolution and assured them that they would enjoy the same rights as men.[21] In the case of the ayatollah, *ketman* succeeded beyond his expectations! As I have already indicated, *ketman* is far from being the clergy's monopoly; indeed, everybody practices it from the bazaar merchant to the highest ranking politician, including the clergy and the shahs. In the early

1960s, in Paris, I was present at the meeting of Muhammad Reza Pahlavi with French orientalists. He charmed them and, after they left, turned to his ambassador in France and said with a grin of satisfaction, "Didn't I fool them well!" A collaborator of Ayatollah Kashani (president of parliament in 1952) told me that he witnessed Prime Minister Mossadegh dancing in his bedroom after having received the French ambassador and repeating joyfully, "I tricked him. I tricked him!"[22]

After Khomeini's triumph and the establishment of his authoritarian theocracy, some of his former secular allies who fled to Europe and America seriously accused him and the mullahs of having diverted the revolution from its liberal and democratic path. They should have known better: indeed, as Iranians they were aware of *ketman*. In the last days of 1978, the mullahs and their followers had already invaded the ranks of demonstrators and their slogans replaced those of the secular opponents. Clearly and openly they chanted: "We reject all political groups, we want Allah's government.... We are against parties. Our party is *Hezbollah* (Party of God).... Our religion is Husseini (allusion to the Prophet's grandson martyred in Kerbela), our king is Khomeini.... Our party is *Hezbollah*, our Shah is Ruhollah (Khomeini's first name)." They made not the slightest allusion to democracy and freedoms! And in February of 1979, when the old ayatollah returned from exile, he was dubbed Imam. It was too late to protest.

CHAPTER FOUR

Tradition vs. Modernization

In the last pages of the preceding chapter I alluded to the role of liberal and secular elements in the Iranian 1979 revolution. Indeed, they were the first to start the protests against the Shah's regime, but far from asking for a return to traditional ways of life they favored modernist reforms. While criticizing the economic and social measures edicted under the so-called White Revolution, they did not oppose them per se. Their demands concerned rather democracy and individual and political freedoms. Ayatollah Khomeini and his followers, to the contrary, did not care for human rights. Their only concern was the reestablishment of traditional institutions and the removal of all modernist reforms accomplished since the early 1960s under the Shah. The old ayatollah played his cards very shrewdly by using *ketman* (deception) in order to pull wool over the liberals' eyes and create dissension in their ranks. Once the Shah fled the country and he triumphantly returned from exile, Khomeini showed his hidden trump cards. From this standpoint, one can see another dimension of the Islamic revolution to which I have already alluded in chapter two: it constitutes one episode in the struggle that has pitched the forces of modernization against those of tradition since the second half of the nineteenth century.

TRADITION VERSUS MODERNIZATION

It was indeed by mid-nineteenth century that an advanced and aggressive West loomed large at the horizon of Islamic countries in general and Iran in particular. Nassereddin Shah paid a state visit to England and France. Wealthy Iranians travelled to Europe and brought back with them some liberal ideas, among which the most important concerned the revolutionary concept of a *constitutional monarchy*. The Iranian shahs since time immemorial were absolute rulers governing with divine sanction. They obviously would not relinquish even a small parcel of their authority. Yet, in 1905, a shaky alliance of some aristocrats, feudal landowners, liberal elements, and high-ranking clergymen resented the autocratic rule of the Qajar kings and succeeded in imposing a constitution on the ailing Mozafareddin Shah. But the latter's successor, Mohammad Shah, with the help of the Russians, arrested the members of the newly elected parliament and reestablished the absolutist regime.

Because of the weakness of the central government in those days, foreign powers intervened in Iran's domestic affairs. The country had even been divided in 1907 into two spheres of influence between the Russians in the North and the British in the South (where the latter were exploiting the oil fields). Backed by the British, the constitutionalist coalition fought back and forced Mohammad Shah to abdicate in favor of his son Ahmad. World

War I interrupted the whole process, as the country was occupied by the Russians, the British, and even the Ottomans. The 1917 Bolshevik Revolution and the 1918 armistice changed the situation in the sense that the British remained as the only influence and tried to become the protectors of Iran by suggesting a draconian treaty in 1919. Some corrupt politicians and aristocrats already on their payroll agreed to recommend its ratification to the parliament. A chaotic situation reigned in the whole country where feudal landowners practically ruled in their latifundia and did not implement the laws adopted by the parliament, nevertheless, the majority of the deputies refused to approve the 1919 treaty with Britain. By 1921, things were completely out of hand and once again a politician manipulated by the British, *seyed* Zia-o-Din Tabatabai, entered Tehran with Reza Khan, the colonel of the cossack brigade, and performed a coup d'état. He was nominated prime minister but was ousted after 100 days in power and replaced by his War Minister Reza Khan.

In 1925 the Qajars were deposed. Reza Khan became Shah and founded the Pahlavi dynasty. The new king, an admirer of Ataturk, started a program of reforms which created modern institutions: civil laws and tribunals, elementary and high schools, universities, police force, hospitals, modern army, railways, and so on. The parliament was kept as a front: the deputies were elected with the Shah's approval. The constitution remained in limbo until the fall of the dynasty in 1979, except for short periods (1942–46 during the occupation of the country by Allied armies; 1950–53 during Mossadegh's premiership). Khomeini abolished it and replaced it through a referendum by a theocratic one.

World War II interrupted the implementation of Reza Shah's reforms. The king was forced by the Allies to abdicate in favor of his son Muhammad Reza Shah. The feudals and the clergy retrieved their past power and dominated the parliament for some time. In the late 1940s, a popular nationalistic movement was organized in order to oust the British from Iran and nationalize the oil industry. Curiously enough, its leader, Dr. Muhammad Mossadegh, was himself an aristocrat and a wealthy landlord. The Shah reluctantly named him prime minister in 1951, but dismissed him in 1953 through a coup performed with the help of the CIA. Under pressure from the Americans, the Shah started his own comprehensive program of modernization which he dubbed White Revolution. The central piece of this program was a land reform which, despite its shortcomings, succeeded in wresting power from the feudal landlords and tribal chiefs. The government was handed to a team of technocrats who were able to build up a solid economic infrastructure in a very short time. But, as indicated in the first chapter, Ayatollah Khomeini's Islamic revolution stopped the development programs and wiped out most of the reforms (for instance, women's equality with men). The feudal landowners did not regain their former power and had to bow to the clerics who did not hesitate to put some of them to death.

In light of the above remarks, one can consider the 1979 rise of Khomeini and his mullahs as one more episode in the battle of tradition versus modernization that has been ongoing in Iran since the middle of the nineteenth century. Each time the modernizers started a program of development capable of pulling the country out of the middle ages, the reactionary feudals, allied with the most extremist part of the clergy and with the bazaar merchants, succeeded in thwarting their efforts; they wielded the real power while pretending to follow the instructions of a government nominated by a weak Shah without real clout. The only difference today lies in the fact that the fundamentalist clergy has abolished monarchy and expelled from the top all other groups, monopolizing decision making at their own behest.

To Iranians and some foreign observers, this succession of defeats suffered by modernizers over more than a century appears as the result of some sort of a spell or curse cast over the Iranian people by a mysterious adverse force. In the fall of 1979, less than a year after the foundation of the Islamic Republic, a Western diplomat posted in Tehran confided to a French journalist, "It seems to me that a fatality [fate?] hangs over this nation."[1] He was watching from his office window the annual Ashura procession in commemoration of the martyrdom of Hussein, the grandson of the Prophet. Hundreds of men were marching, chanting, weeping, and flagellating themselves. The diplomat had the impression that misfortune was dogging the country and forbidding it to come out of its remote past. While he was right on the face of it, he probably ignored the deep-seated unconscious mechanisms that motivated the people and therefore could not understand that actually, Iranians themselves had forged the fate that pursued them!

As some historians and psychologists have remarked, people of each epoch need a reference to a former era in which they can find justification for their present life and also reassuring models with which to conform. Thus, for instance, since World War II, the Muslims in general and the Arabs in particular look back at what they call their golden age. They usually place it at the zenith of the Abbasid Caliphate, when Baghdad's splendors fascinated Charlemagne and the backward Westerners. In this respect, Iranians can refer to several golden ages. Their remotest legends, shared with other Indo-Europeans, speak of a paradise lost, a lush abode which evil forces (Ahriman in the case of Iranians) suddenly transformed into an icy region, forcing them to migrate. They can also turn toward the times of Zoroaster, who brought the spiritual message of Ahura Mazda, and Cyrus, who founded a great model empire. Finally, they can look at Ali's short-lived caliphate and at the teachings of the Imams, the last of whom disappeared in his infancy. Therefore, one should not be nonplused by Ayatollah Khomeini's incertitute; indeed, he referred sometimes to the governments of the Prophet and Ali (seventh century), and other times to a political and judicial organization reminding one of the Seljukid rule and Ghazali's theology (end of the eleventh century) or the Almohads and Ibn Tumart's fundamentalism (second half of the twelfth century); not counting his appeals to pre-Islamic Iranian patriotism during the war with Iraq (the Islamic official radio dubbed the first victory against Iraqi invaders as revenge for the battle of Qadissiah which marked the defeat of the Sassanids and the rise of Islam in Iran!). Notwithstanding these diverse references, it must be said that in Khomeini's mind the real golden age was that period of Islam which he qualified as the time of perfection, meaning the short span of time during which the Prophet ruled in Medina. As a Shiite, Khomeini thought that after Ali's assassination, the Arabs betrayed the teachings of Islam by creating hereditary monarchies and stopping the jihad (holy war). That treason triggered the decline and caused the decadence of Muslim countries. To retrieve their past splendor and prosperity, Muslims should therefore revert to what was going on during the time of perfection and revive the conditions and major events of their religion's beginnings.

In a way this reminds one, aggrandized to the scale of a whole nation, of the psychoanalysts' efforts to bring back to consciousness what they call the primal scene. But instead of retrieving it through free associations, fundamentalists propose to reject all institutions and ways of life inspired by the West and to revert to literal Koranic teachings and the Prophet Suna's prescriptions. This in turn reminds one of what the late Professor Mircea Eliade called *the myth of the eternal return*, according to which whatever happened in sacred times (the beginnings) can be recreated and repeated by the dint of rites and paradigms. In his book bearing the same title, Professor Eliade noted that in archaic or premodern societies, people believed that by returning to the remotest past man could reestablish his lost links with divinity.

Be this as it may, in Iran of the 1960s, to be sure, Khomeini was not the only one to evince a strong nostalgia for the remote past. His mortal nemesis, the Shah, too, thought about returning to primeval times. But his golden age differed from that of Khomeini and appeared as an even more curious cocktail. Indeed, it referred to both Cyrus and Zoroaster on the one hand, and to the Prophet of Islam and the Saint Imams on the other! At the same time the Shah yearned for Western rationalism, science, and technology, thus aggravating his contradictions.

Caught in the vise of all these conflicting views and goals, the Iranians seemed somehow bewildered. They also had their own nostalgias. As Freud once noted: "Remote times have a great attraction—sometimes mysteriously so—for the imagination. As often as mankind is dissatisfied with its present—and that happens often enough—it harks back to the past and hopes at last to win belief in the never forgotten dream of a Golden Age."[2]

By 1978, discontent was almost general. To some the reforms were too rapid, to others too slow. The mushrooming of private modern banks stole a march on bazaar merchants who used to perform financial operations and give loans (often at extremely high interest). The concentration of most businesses in the hands of a minority orbiting around the members of the royal family enraged all those who wanted to get their share of the pie. Inflation and soaring prices ate away salaries. Agribusiness around the big dams was not welcome by peasants to whom shares were given: in their view, valueless paper replaced their lands. The intelligentsia resented censorship and repression. The growing middle class wanted a greater participation in the political leadership. The clergy's influence and income were diminishing. With the exception of the farmers, almost everybody was complaining for some reason.[3]

Modernization and economic improvement were somehow adversely sensed by heads of families; fathers, for instance, felt anger at the ways their children tended to disobey them. In addition, a kind of metaphysical void was developing in many sectors of the population. The new values proposed to the public (such as, for instance, the resurrection of past splendors) did not jibe with the democratic aspirations of the educated people. To the middle class, the economic goals could not replace religious beliefs. The Shah's mind, clouded by his delusions of grandeur, could not understand the fact that the modern technology he longed for was not neutral: it came with democratic ideologies attached to it. These technologies were born in a completely secular atmosphere of separation of church and state and the image of the universe they propagated was devoid of a hereafter. They reduced messianism, as it were, to simple social welfare. They did not care about life after death, but entered into an environment which was still medieval and, through a stultified theology, gave more importance to the other world![4]

In short, the Shah, like many Third World dictators, considered modernization as a mere material process consisting of the impor-

tation of technology. He did not sense, beyond †
vanced contrivances and the exuberance of new
sity of *ideological reforms*, the urgency of bring
the mind-set of the people. He did not underst
did not boil down to factories, consumer goods, new ⸢⸤
tertainment, and more permissive manners. He would not admit
that modernity was first and foremost a whole new philosophy up-
holding the basic dignity and freedoms of human beings.

Indeed, anybody having the means can buy in any corner of the
planet machines, radios, television sets, computers, and the like.
Thus, the Iranian mullahs and other fundamentalists, despite their
antimodernist rhetoric, travel in jets, use cassettes and tapes to
spread their propaganda, speak through cellular phones, gorge
themselves with vitamins, call Western surgeons to operate on
their ailing ayatollahs and sheikhs, buy rockets and nuclear ingre-
dients. In other words, they do not spurn any of the satanic inventions of the much-hated West. Yet they do not become modern and
could not develop or partake in a scientific and technological environment!

The mistake of Iranian (and probably other Third World) modernizers lies in the fact that they thought that development could
be accomplished by following gradual steps: first the infrastructure
(material basis) and then the superstructure (democracy). I remember the discussions in the United Nations about the two
covenants on human rights. The Third World countries and the
Soviet group would give priority to the economic one over the political. They argued that you have first to feed the people, otherwise
they would die. They proposed to postpone the covenant on political rights. Well, experience tends to prove that all rights have the
same importance. Indeed, one cannot separate the mind from the

dy. Even a hungry man, primitive or modern, has metaphysical needs.

To come back to the events in Iran, one can say that the majority of the population was steeped in a kind of funk by 1978. Naturally obsessed with the past, they were unable to imagine the future. The changes already brought by the economic and social development frightened them. The Shah and the upper crust of society, generally nonpracticing Muslims, looked toward the remote past and nurtured a kind of, so to say, populist nationalism based on dreams built with elements borrowed from the history of the Achaemenian and Sassanid periods. The middle classes, bazaar merchants, and the lower classes, still influenced by the clerics, looked also toward the past, but a relatively recent one linked to the values of Shiism, not those of defunct empires. Yet another group, more or less prone to scientific and rational thinking, longed for a democratic system based on civil society.

In the 1970s, almost every Iranian longed for a golden age, located in the past or in the future, but these golden ages were far from being the same. For Khomeini it was the Islamic government of the Prophet in Medina and Ali in Koufa, for the Shah, the imperial reign of Cyrus, for the intellectuals, a democratic government based on political freedoms and human rights. Moreover, each one of them pursued goals which were mixed with elements borrowed from the others. Thus the clerics, while wanting to resuscitate the government of the Prophet and Ali, yearned for the most advanced technology, ignoring the fact that it contained the seeds of secularism; in the same manner the Shah desired modernization without its democratic features; and the intellectuals fancied keeping intact their ancient culture in a modern democracy! They all lived, and continue to live, in a state of continual self-delusion. These golden ages are nothing but dreams projected toward the past or the future.

Having placed Khomeini's Islamic revolution in the context of the ongoing battle between traditionalists and modernists and having defined its objectives, it becomes possible to predict its future demise: one cannot swim against the flow of history and go back to the past. A similar remark applies to the Shah's dream of resuscitating the glories of Cyrus and Darius. As for the intellectuals and liberals and their democratic wishes, they must remember that they cannot go to their desired future carrying the heavy baggage of their 2000-year-old culture. All traditionalists and modernizers, should resist their utopian drives and come down to earth and its present realities.

Indeed, it seems that Iranians, despite all their sophistication, education, and progress, remain nevertheless entangled in their own traditions and mythologies. They know what they want. They figure out the ways to reach their goals. But they seem incapable of acting without the guidance of a fatherly leader. Curiously enough, the leader almost always fails to live up to their expectations. To limit ourselves to the twentieth century, Reza Shah, Mossadegh, Muhammad Reza Shah, Ayatollah Khomeini, and now President Khatami, one after another, disappointed their supporters.

A SAVIOR?

Yet, after more than two millennia of repetitive frustration, the utopian dream of a strong father or savior as perpetuated by legends and mythologies as well as religions (Feridun, Rostam, Shoshyant in Zoroastrianism) remains alive and operational in Iran. It still is one of the unconscious forces that drive social and political upheavals and movements.

The mechanism of this tendency, which constitutes a real *syndrome* in behavior of Iranians is perfectly described in the legend of Jamshid and Zahak. If one looks back at the details of this mythical story, one finds that the real architects of Ahriman's defeat are, first and foremost, Ahura Mazda acting through the blacksmith Kaveh, and then, the people themselves, the masses. Feridun, the savior, is brought back from Damavand *after* Kaveh's confrontation with Zahak, not before! He actually performs nothing practical. He is just the triggerer, the element that responds to the belief of the people in the necessity of a savior. He replaces Zahak on the throne after the latter's overthrow, but all the groundwork, as it were, is accomplished by Kaveh and the people themselves. The so-called savior is in fact a kind of will-ò-the-wisp, a kind of deceptive goal.

It seems that Iranians, no matter how educated and sincere in their desire for change, stay prisoners of their own traditional mythology. What they need is neither an Islamic nor a White revolution, but rather a cultural one. It is true that Mao's mid-1960s bloody utopia has smeared the very concept of cultural revolutions, but I don't find a better phrase to characterize what we need in Iran. In hindsight, I think that Mao's error was his idea to altogether wipe out the cultural past of his country. As one cannot travel back into the past, one cannot either cut all links with established traditions! At any stage of history, large chunks of the national past accompany people. Each nation must therefore constantly construct medleys of their past and present as they advance on the highways of the future.

In short, one can neither revive the past nor erase it completely. Does this mean that Iranians are condemned to run forever inside the vicious circle of their traditions without any hope of freeing themselves? Shall they eternally jump from secular dictatorships into theocratical ones and vice versa? I do not think so. To the contrary, I believe that they have at their disposal an easy and inexpensive way of escaping once and for all from their predicament. In order to convey my idea with minimum development, I resort to a metaphor borrowed from the technologies of the early twentieth century. I am sure that even younger generations still remember the gramophones of yesteryear with their grooved playing records. In that perspective the repetitive trends of Iranian history remind one of a record with spoiled grooves that keeps repeating the same notes and words. The most efficient way to remedy this annoyance consisted in replacing the record. Is such a medicine available in the case of Iran's present problem? I, for one, answer affirmatively.

I indicated in chapter two the way in which mythology and tradition continue to influence and determine the behavior and actions of Iranians. I have shown the remarkable similarities between the legend of Jamshid and Zahak and the Iranian cycles of power. I have also elaborated about the dominant characteristics of the Iranian father-ruler and his legendary model, Rostam the superman. Finally, I have pointed out how these two mythological stories are implanted in the brains of children and youngsters by mothers, nannies, and public storytellers.

The first hints of a possible solution dawned on me, a couple of years ago, when I was rereading Plato in an English translation. A passage of *The Republic* struck me, in which the great philosopher spoke about the influence of fables on children and societies. He told parents and educators: "Choose the good fables and dismiss the bad. We will instruct the nannies and the mothers to tell the children these chosen tales ... in order to change the souls.... Most of those they are telling now should be rejected."[5]

Fortunately, Iranians possess a vast and variegated mythology in which they might find beautiful stories in accord with their present needs. Among them, one appears to me extremely timely, considering what is happening now inside Iran and in the world at large. It is the legend of the exemplary king Kaykhosrow, who, at the peak of his reign decided to abandon power and retire in the mountains. He had achieved great deeds and faithfully served both God and his people. He had defeated the enemies of Iran and ensured the security of all its provinces, as well as the prosperity and happiness of his people. Instead of sinking, like Jamshid, into self-satisfaction and hubris, he thought that the time had come for him to retire and pass the scepter to someone else. He therefore assembled his collaborators and the people and told them about his intentions. All Iranians, who were appreciative of his achievements, pleaded with him. They beseeched him to abandon his project. He did not yield to their entreaties. Instead, he told them that he feared that by remaining longer at the top, he would unintentionally do things that would displease them and God. In his beautiful verses, Ferdowsi suggests that the ruler became sated with kingship and worried about the hereafter; the poet shows Kaykhosrow in meditation, praying to God:

> O higher than the highest, show to me
>   The ways of righteousness and purity;
>   Guide me to heaven, let me leave behind
>   This fleeting habitation of mankind,

And let my heart shun sin, so that I might
Pass to the realms of everlasting light.[6]

In Ferdowsi's rendition of the legend, a number of great heroes accompany their beloved king on the slopes of Damavand mountain and rest near a stream.

And when the dawn's light touched their resting place
The king had gone, leaving no earthly trace.

The occultation of Kaykhosrow has nurtured popular beliefs, according to which the king did not die, but went into hiding and would return.[7] Be this as it may, I find it difficult to agree TODAY with Ferdowsi's interpretation of the legend. Indeed, I think that people should, at each stage of their history, *revisit* their mythologies in the light of the newly acquired knowledge and in relation to their needs.[8] Ferdowsi's reading of Iranian pre-Islamic mythology certainly had solid grounds and important significations for his time. Yet his epic masterpiece might yield in our epoch *new interpretations* beyond its apparent story lines. Even in Ferdowsi's version, I, for one, think that what Kaykhosrow wanted to convey to his people was the necessity of limiting the duration of leadership for the sake of good governance. His was a *lesson in democracy.* Many features of the legend catch our attention now that younger Iranian generations are fighting for an open and civil society. For instance, Kaykhosrow had no heirs: a new king had to be *chosen.* The legend can therefore be interpreted, among other things, as a rejection of hereditary monarchy. To be sure, one can also find many other significations in Kaykhosrow's story. For the purpose of this chapter, I limit myself to the aspects concerning governance. In this perspective, one can say that democratic principles existed in Iranian traditions.

It is obvious that in an environment of absolutism, Ferdowsi couldn't insist on the political implications of the legend, especially since the *Shahnameh* had been commissioned by Shah Mahmoud! This also explains why Kaykhosrow's story is not told to children like the legends of Jamshid and Rostam, which favor absolute leaders, kings, and fathers. Getting back to the aforementioned Plato's advice, I would suggest that the use of Kaykhosrow's legend as a children's bedtime story might help in breaking up the vicious cycle in which Iranians have been caught over so many centuries.

Notes

Preface

1. Importance of mythology in the conduct of people.

The contemporary philosopher Alastair MacIntyre once said that people are "storytelling animals"; he added that people become possessed by stories that orient them in the world. Indeed, to many modern historians the "fictions" of a society contribute as fundamentally to its character as its laws and political and economic arrangements (see, for instance, Marina Warner, cultural historian and novelist: *Six Myths of Our Time: Little Angels, Little Monsters, Beautiful Beasts and More*, New York, 1995). The French historian Georges Duby who specializes in medieval societies, for his part, insisted on the importance of tracking the "mental representations of people" in order to understand their actions (*Des Sociétés Médiévales*, Paris, 1970). Claude Levy Strauss in his eulogy of Georges Dumézil as a new member of the French Academy, said, "The secret of men's actions is to be found in the myths they have created."

Anthropologists, sociologists, and psychologists go even further in establishing the importance of myths. Professor Richard Sennett remarked that myths are ideas people need to believe in, whether they are true or not; all societies from the primitive to the overcivilized are held together by such ideas (*The Fall of Public Man*, New York, 1976).

Professor Elemire Zolla stated that we "are ruled not by Reason but by manifestations of primeval patterns: archetypes" and "archetypes pervade mythology" (*The Persistence of Unifying Patterns*, New York, 1982). Professor John Hinnells affirmed that, "Not only are myths expressions of man's reflection on the basic meaning of life, they are also charters by which he lives, and they can act as the rationale of a society" (*Persian Mythology*, New York, 1985). Erich Fromm, speaking of the revival of the myth of Oedipus in psychotherapy, wrote in 1948 that both myths and dreams use "symbolic language" which is the only "common language" of the human race; he remarked: "All great cultures of the past regarded symbolic language and hence myths and dreams as highly significant. . . . The understanding of symbols became an art which had an important cultural function. But while we all continued to 'speak' the language in our dreams, we forgot its meaning, much to the detriment of our insight into the past of the human race and into the depths of our own experience. . . . The myth, like the dream, is the 'regal road' to the understanding of unconscious processes, as Freud put it; psychoanalysis is 'the' method of understanding these creations of man's unconscious"; he added that psychoanalysis could "break" the secret code of myths (Introduction to *Oedipus, Myth and Complex: A Review of Psychoanalytic Theory*, by Patrick Mullahy, New York, 1948).

I must also recall in this respect all the works of Mircea Eliade who demonstrated the survival of myths, especially in traditional societies. For him, the myths "preserve and transmit the paradigms, the exemplary models, for all the responsible activities in which men engage" (see all of Eliade's books on myths and especially *The Myth of the Eternal Return*, paperback, Princeton, 1974) which he considered as the most significant of all his works).

2. "The Ideology of the Way of Life in the Indian Epic (Mahabharata and Ramayana) and its Reflection in Early Sanskrit Drama," lecture delivered by Professor Emeritus Khosrow D. Irani at City College, New York (Amsterdam Avenue at 137th Street, October 12, 1995).

3. André Malraux, "Anti-memoires" III, 1 in *Miroir des Limbes*, edition "La Pleiade" (Paris, 1976).

4. Ginzburg continued: "I am very conscious that my attraction for witches and werewolves goes back to those first books. That's why I am against the idea of protecting children from scary tales or stories that can

unlock imagination. I read them to my own daughters when they were very young." excerpted from "Was the World Made out of Cheese?" by Jonathan Kandell, *New York Times Magazine*, November 17, 1991.

5. Over the years, even when as a diplomat I was involved in negotiations for reaching compromises among opposed views, I became gradually convinced that although living on the same planet, nations were far from being contemporary with one another. They were at different stages of development. Thus for instance in the Middle East conflict, no lasting peace would be possible without some changes in the mind-sets of the people on both sides. (See my articles in "American Foreign Policy Interests" and my books: *L'Islam Bloqué* (Paris 1993) and *The Broken Crescent* (Westport, Connecticut, 1998).

Chapter 1: The Shah and the Ayatollah

1. Many Muslim leaders, religious as well as secular, have spent all or part of their childhood and adolescence in the care of an uncle (or aunt). Egypt's Nasser, for instance, while in Cairo for his school attendance, lived with his uncle. Iraq's Saddam Hussein was sent to his uncle in Baghdad for a similar reason. Khomeini's case is even more impressive because he was orphaned and left in the care of his aunt and her husband. Very often militant biographers have invented such an uncle-nephew relationship for their leaders. It is significant for Muslim "great men" to have been orphaned or at least separated from their biological parents. Indeed the Prophet Muhammad was orphaned in his infancy and brought up by his uncle. And in the Muslim world, the Prophet is offered as as a supreme saintly model. Since childhood every believer has learned the details of his life. Consequently the notions of "orphan" and "uncle custody" conjure up the memory of the Prophet and provoke immediate sympathy and affection. Moreover, in the Middle East any coincidence or parallel with legendary or real heroes is considered as a heavenly sign and interpreted as a good omen. It also often happens that some youths, more sensitive and impressionable than others, who are living with their uncles, come to believe that they are predestined to accomplish great deeds. I have coined the phrase "uncle syndrome" to explain, at least partially, the mechanism of the rise of charismatic leaders and the profound devotion of their followers.

2. *Badghadam* (of bad omen); *khoshghadam* (of good omen); these "superstitions" are nurtured by "ways of thinking" or "logics" that one (following Mircea Eliade and others) can characterize as "archaic or pre-modern". The people of traditional societies establish a direct cause and effect relationship between the birth of a child and what happens to his father and family in the aftermath of his or her birth.

3. People avoided Khomeini as a child because of what has been explained in the above note 2; thinking in the framework of the same "logic" they were afraid that the "bad omen" would affect them too!

4. R.K. Karanjia, *The Mind of a Monarch* (London, 1977).

5. In the French magazine *Confidences*, number 1094 (Paris, 1968).

6. Cyrus Ghani, *Iran and the Rise of Reza Shah: From Qajar Collapse to Pahlavi Power* (London, 1998).

7. Amir Taheri, *The Spirit of Allah* (New York, 1986).

8. Reza Shah, the father of Muhammad Reza Shah, introduced the compulsory use of family names. He himself chose the name Pahlavi, after the appellation of the Iranian language of the Zoroastrian literature.

9. Karanjia, *The Mind of a Monarch*.

10. Ibid.

11. Ibid.

12. Ibid.

13. The question was asked by Paul Balta, a French journalist (*Le Monde*) who had been invited by Khomeini's staff to accompany the ayatollah on his trip back to Iran.

14. Taheri, *The Spirit of Allah*.

15. *Unveiling the Secrets.*

16. Deceiving infidels was allowed, if not encouraged, by all Muslims. Shiites extended the dissimulation even to believers whenever the secutity of their "cause" was at stake. For further details on the use of dissimulation (*ketman*) by Iranian clerics, see Gobineau, *Trois Ans en Asie*, and my book: *The Broken Crescent* (Westport, CT, 1998).

17. Olivier Warin, *Le Leon et le Soleil* (Paris, 1976).

18. Karanjia, *The Mind of a Monarch*.

19. Muhammad Reza Pahlavi, *Toward the Great Civilization* (Tehran, 1978).

20. Ibid.

21. Karanjia, *The Mind of a Monarch*.

22. Ibid.

23. Fereydoun Hoveyda, *The Fall of the Shah* (New York, 1980).

24. Between the 7th and 11th centuries Muslim clerics and their interpretations of the Koran and Islamic law were less rigid. Muslims in general and their scholars in particular opened themselves to foreign cultures (Persian, Greek, etc). See my books: *The Broken Crescent* and *L'Islam Bloqué*.

25. *Le Monde Diplomatique* (April 1979).

26. Pahlavi, *Toward the Great Civilization*.

27. *Le Monde Diplomatique* (April 1979).

28. *Kayhan* (Iran, June 11, 1976).

Chapter 2: The Enduring Mythology of Persia

1. René Grousset and Georges Deniker, *La Face de l'Asie* (Paris, 1955).

2. Pahlavi, *Toward the Great Civilization*.

3. Mircea Eliade, *The Myth of the Eternal Return* (Princeton, 1954).

4. "We know how, in the past, humanity has been able to endure the sufferings we have enumerated: they were regarded as punishment inflicted by God, the syndrome of the decline of the 'age', and so on. And it was possible to accept them precisely because they had a metahistorical meaning, because, for the greater part of mankind, still clinging to the traditional viewpoint, history did not have, and could not have, value in itself. Every hero repeated the archetypal gesture, every war rehearsed the struggle between good and evil, every fresh social injustice was identified with the sufferings of the Saviour ... , each new massacre repeated the glorious end of the martyrs" (Mircea Eliade, *The Myth of the Eternal Return*, first paperback edition (Princeton, 1971, page 151).

5. See, for instance, Mircea Eliade, *The Myth of the Eternal Return* (Princeton, 1954 and 1971) and *Aspects du Mythe* (Paris, 1963).

6. H.S. Nyberg, "Questions de Cosmologie et Cosmogonie Mazdeennes" in *Journal Asiatique 219* (Paris, July 1931).

7. Gobineau, *Trois Ans en Asie*, Part 2, chapter 1.

8. Ehsan Yarshater, "Ta'ziyeh and Pre-Islamic Mourning Rites in Iran" in *Ta'ziyeh: Ritual and Drama in Iran*, edited by Peter Chelkowski (New York, 1979).

9. Ibid.

10. Eliade, *The Myth of the Eternal Return.*

11. Georges Dumezil, *Mitra—Varuna: Essai sur Deux Representations Indo-Europeennes de la Souveraineté;* (Paris, 1948).

12. *Fathers and Sons: Stories From the Shahnameh of Ferdowsi,* vol 2, trans. Dick Davis (Washington, DC, 2000).

13. In the French Revolution, mobs marched on Versailles Palace; in the Russian Revolution, crowds invaded the Winter Palace; and so on.

14. Pahlavi, *Toward the Great Civilization.*

15. F. Hoveyda, *My Last Audience with the Shah* (memoir, in my Internet site and in the Iranian).

16. Khomeini's interviews and declarations in Neauphle-le-Chateau, France.

17. Ibid.

18. Tanzar's letter to the King of Tabaristan in Gerard Walter, *Le Memorial des Siecles; IIIeme Siecle; Les evenements, La Montée des Sassanides* by Jean Gagé (Paris, 1964).

19. India's "Caste System" is fully inspired by the tripartite ideology.

20. On the triumph of fundamentalism and the start of decline in the twelfth century, see my books: *L'Islam Bloqué* and *The Broken Crescent.*

21. Hoveyda, *The Broken Crescent,* chapter 6.

22. Ibid.

23. The historian Ibn Khaldun in the fourteenth century; the mathematicain Ibn Massud in the fifteenth century; etc.

24. See chapter 4.

25. Khomeini's speech on Tehran radio on August 24, 1979.

26. René Grousset and G. Deniker, *La Face de l'Asie* (Paris, 1955).

27. Plato, "Choose the good fables and dismiss the bad.…" in *The Republic,* vol. 2 (377b).

Chapter 3: The Unwritten Constitution and the "Hidden Imam"

1. Paul Balta and Claudine Rulleau, *L'Iran Insurgé* (Paris, 1979).

2. Amir Taheri, *The Spirit of Allah* (New York, 1986).

3. Ali is the first Imam, his elder son Hassan, the second; his second son, Hussein, the third. The other Imams, descendants of Hussein, are: Zaynalabeddin (fourth); Muhammad Baqir (fifth); Jafar Sadiq (sixth);

Mussa Kazim (seventh); Ali Reza (eighth); Muhammad Javad (ninth); Ali Hadi (tenth); Hassan Askari (eleventh); Muhammad Muntazar, the *Mahdi*, the Hidden Imam (twelfth).

4. The most important Shiite sect after the "Twelfthers" is called "Ismailism" whose leaders created an independent Caliphate in Cairo (909–1160); Ismailism ends the Imams at the seventh who is actually different in the Twelfthers' doctrine. Indeed, the sixth Imam, Jafar Sadiq, had two sons; the elder (Ismail) died five years before his father and had been "discharged" by him because of a bout of drinking and nominated the second (Kazim) as his official heir. The majority of Shiites accepted Kazim as their seventh Imam, but a number of believers rejected the decision of the father and considered Ismail as their seventh Imam; Ismail had no children. The present leader of the Ismailism is the Agha Khan. There are also numerous other Shiite sects. Some considered Ali as the most important Imam; some faded away; others survived as very small communities.

5. Gobineau, *Trois Ans en Asie*.

6. Pahlavi, *Toward the Great Civilization*.

7. See Chapter 1.

8. Ruhollah Khomeini, *Velayt-e-Faghih*. Published by his students under the title: *Hokoumat-e-Islami* (Islamic government).

9. Michel Foucault, for instance, hailed in 1979 the Islamic revolution and affirmed that Khomeini introduced a "spiritual dimension into politics" (See *Le Nouvel Observateur*, number 727). Professor Richard Falk (Princeton) went as far as writing that Khomeini would profer a model of "humanistic" government for the Third World (*The New York Times*, February 27, 1984). Professor Falk also said that the Islamic Republic would be an "element of stability" in the Persian Gulf and Middle East (*Foreign Policy*, number 34, spring 1979).

10. Ruhollah Khomeini, *Kashf-ol-Asrar* (The Disclosing of the Secrets).

11. Khomeini, *Hokoumat-e-Islami* (Islamic government).

12. Quoted by Paul Balta in *L'Iran Insurgé*.

13. Here lies the origin of the slogan "Islam in danger."

14. Declaration from the Iranian daily *Ettelaat*, October 25, 1978.

15. *Ettelaat*, August 18, 1979.

16. *Ettelaat*, November 9, 1978.

17. *Qum*, October 22, 1979.

18. C. Bernard and C. Khalilzad, *The Government of God* (New York, 1984).

19. *Le Monde* (January 31, 1979).

20. Gobineau, *La Religion et la Philosophie dans l'Asie Centrale*, chapter 1.

21. Quoted by Paul Balta, *L'Iran Insurgé*.

22. Reported by Ehsan Naraghi, a collaborator of Ayatollah Kashani.

Chapter 4: Tradition vs. Modernization

1. As told to me by Eric Rouleau, a French journalist.

2. Sigmund Freud, *Moses and Monotheism* New York, 1957:89–90. Freud continues: "Probably man still stands under the magic spell of his childhood, which a not unbiased memory presents to him as a time of unalloyed bliss. Incomplete and dim memories of the past, which we call *tradition*, are a great incentive to the artist, for he is free to fill in the gaps in the memories according to the behests of his imagination and to form after his own purpose the image of the time he has undertaken to reproduce. One might almost say that the more shadowy tradition has become, the more meat is for the poet's use."

3. Reinhold Loeffler: "For the first time in their history they (the peasants of Boir Ahmad and Kuhgiluyeh, in Southern Iran) (in the mid-1970s) saw a light at the end of the tunnel of old-age poverty. And they credit the Shah for it. They credit the Shah for the land-reform, they credit him for the conditions that gave them the possibility to earn salaries and to do wage-labor in the towns, and they credit him with the resultant economic upsurge of their livelihoods.... From the outset they were very skeptical about the (Islamic) revolution.... For them, with the revolution, there was an abrupt halt in the upsurge, and as a consequence they feel anger and frustration with the regime.... They publicly express their discontent, by, for instance boycotting the religious rituals.... This going even so far as to affect the observance of their private rituals such as praying and fasting...." (in *Revolution and the Islamic Republic*.

4. The importance given by Shiite Islamic theology to the hereafter over the present life on earth and its influence on believers can be seen in the droves of "candidates" to "martyrdom" during the eight years' war with Iraq.

5. Plato, *The Republic*, vol 2 (377b).

6. *Fathers and Sons*, trans. Dick Davis.

7. The "Hidden Imam" reminds one of the "hidden saviour" in Iranian ancient mythology (for instance Feridun of Jamshid and Zahak legend, is "hidden" in Damavand mountain). This is indeed a well-entrenched feature in the mind-set of Iranians.

8. In my opinion it is absolutely necessary for Iranians to "revisit" and "reinterpret" their old mythology and legends (both religious and non-religious) if they want to progress while they retain their cultural identity. Actually, in the advanced democracies of the West such a reinterpretation happens, as it were, "naturally." Indeed scientists, thinkers, and essayists do such revisions in their various research and publications.

Bibliography

Balta, Paul and Rulleau, Claudine. *L'Iran insurgé*. Paris, 1979.

Benard, Cheryl and Khalilzad, Zalmay. *The Government of God: Iran's Islamic Republic*. New York, 1984.

Campbell, Joseph. *Myths to Live By*. New York, 1975.

———. *The Power of Myth*. New York, 1976.

———. *Hero With a Thousand Faces*. New York, 1977.

Carré, Olivier and Dumont, Paul. *Radicalismes Islamiques*. Paris, 1985.

Chelkowski, Peter. *Ta'ziyeh: Ritual and Drama in Iran*. New York, 1978.

Corbin, Henry. *En Islam Iranien*. Paris, 1976.

Davis, Dick. *Fathers and Sons*. Washington, DC, 2000.

Detienne, Marcel. *L'Invention de la Mythologie*. Paris, 1981.

Dumézil, Georges. *Mitra–Varuna: Essai sur Deux Representations Indo-Europeennes de la Souveraineté*. Paris, 1948.

———. *Mythe et Epopee: I-L'Ideologie des Trois Fonctions*. Paris, 1971.

———. *L'Oubli de l'Homme et l'Honneur des Dieux*. Paris, 1985.

Eliade, Mircea. *The Myth of Eternal Return or Cosmos and History*. Princeton, 1954 and 1971.

———. *Aspects du Mythe*. Paris, 1963.

———. *La Nostalgie des Origines*. Paris, 1971.

Fenichel, Otto. *The Psychoanalytic Theory of Neurosis*. New York, 1971.

Fiedler, Leslie. *Freaks: Myths and Images of the Secret Self*. New York, 1978.

Freud, Sigmund. *Moses and Monotheism*. New York, 1957.

———. *Inhibitions, Symptoms and Anxiety*. New York, 1977.

———. *The Basic Writings of Sigmund Freud*. New York, 1995.

Frye, Richard. *The Heritage of Persia*. New York, 1966.

Gagé, Jean. *La Montée des Sassanides*. Paris, 1964.

Ghani, Cyrus. *Iran and the Rise of Reza Shah*. London, 1998.

Gobineau, Arthur de. *Trois ans en Asie*. Paris, 1890.

Goudarzi, Mahmoud. *What Is Mythology?* in "Par" no. 54. (In Persian.)

Gross, John. *Shylock: A Legend and its Legacy*. New York, 1993.

Grousset, René and G. Deniker. *La Face de l'Asie*. Paris, 1945.

Hinnells, John. *Persian Mythology*. New York, 1973 and 1985.

Hoveyda, Fereydoun. *The Fall of the Shah*. New York, 1980.

———. *Les Nuits Feodales*. Paris, 1983.

———. *L'Islam Bloqué*. Paris, 1993.

———. *The Broken Crescent*. Westport, CT, 1998.

Jansen, G.H. *Militant Islam*. London, 1979.

Karanjia, R.K. *The Mind of a Monarch*. London, 1977.

Kedouri, Elie. *Afghani and Abduh*. London, 1966.

Khomeini, Ruhollah. *Unveiling the Secrets*. Tehran 1979. (In Persian.)

———. *Islamic Government*. Tehran 1980. (In Persian.)

———. *Liberation of Means*. Tehran, 1985. (In Persian.)

Kramer, Samuel Noah. *Mythologies of the Ancient World*. New York, 1961.

Lenczowski, George. *Iran Under the Pahlavis*. Stanford, 1977.

Lerner, Daniel. *The Passing of Traditional Society: Modernizing the Middle East*. New York, 1958.

Leven, Steven. *Obsessive-Compulsive Disorders: Treating and Understanding Crippling Habits*. New York, 1992.

Levi-Strauss, Claude. *The Jealous Potter*. New York, 1985.

———. *The Story of Lynx*. New York, 1995.

Lewis, Bernard. *The Jews of Islam*. Princeton, 1982.

Masson, Emilia. *Le Combat de l'Immortalité: Heritage Indo-Europeen dans la Mythologie Anatolienne*. Paris, 1991.

Middleton, John. *Myths and Cosmos: Readings in Mythology and Symbolism*. New York, 1967.

Mohammadi, Mohammad. *Iranian Culture and Its Influence on Islamic Civilization and Arab Literature*. Tehran, 1976. (In Persian.)

Mullahy, Patrick. *Oedipus, Myth and Complex: A Review of Psychoanalytic Theory*. Introduction by Erich Fromm. New York, 1948.

Nagera, H. *Obsessional Neuroses: Developmental Psychopathology*. New York, 1995.

Pahlavi, Mohammad Reza. *Toward the Great Civilization*. Tehran, 1978. (In Persian.)

Pye, Lucian. *Asian Power and Politics*. (especially the chapter: Paternal Authority and Oriental Despotism) New York, 1986.

Robinson, Herbert Spenser and Wilson, Knox. *Myths and Legends of All Nations*. New York, 1950.

Roheim, Geza. *The Origin and Function of Culture*. New York, 1943.

Shay, Jonathan. *Achilles in Vietnam: Combat Trauma and the Undoing of Character*. New York, 1994.

Taheri, Amir. *The Spirit of Allah: Khomeini and the Islamic Revolution*. New York, 1984.

———. *Holy Terror: Inside the World of Islamic Terrorism*. Bethesda, MD, 1987.

Warner, Marina. *Six Myths of Our Time*. New York, 1995.

Zolla, Elemire. *The Persistence of Unifying Patterns*. New York, 1982.

Name Index

Subject Index

About the Author

FEREYDOUN HOVEYDA is a Senior Fellow with the National Committee on American Foreign Policy. He also is a former Iranian Ambassador to the UN (1971–1978). In 1972 and 1973, he chaired the UN Committee on International Terrorism created after the assassination of Israeli athletes at the Olympics in Germany. A widely published author of fiction and nonfiction, his *Les neiges du Sinai* won the Leopold Senghor Award in 1973.